The
SECOND MOUSE
GETS THE **CHEESE**

How to Avoid the Traps
of Self-Publishing

Carolyn P. Schriber

Published by Katzenhaus Books
P. O. Box 1629
Cordova, Tennessee 38088-1629

ISBN: 0982774559
ISBN-13: 9780982774557

Library of Congress Control Number: 20119941962
Katzenhaus Books, Cordova, TN

Table of Contents

FOREWORD:
Changing Times

It was 1981, and I had finished typing my master's thesis. I had used an electric typewriter, but had still struggled with the need to produce three letter-perfect carbon copies. Do you remember what a pain that was? No strikeovers allowed, and erasures needed to be invisible. All footnotes went at the bottom of the page, not the end, and, believe me, a thesis in medieval history has a lot of footnotes. We had an elaborate system of typing a list of all footnotes first, so that we could tell how many lines each one would take. Then, armed with the knowledge of how many lines were available within the margins of a page, we stopped every time a footnote number appeared in the text. We counted the separating line, the space before the note, and the number of lines in the note itself—then subtracted that number from the number of lines available for text. Type another footnote number on the same page? Stop and recalculate. When a fellow student told me about a new-fangled invention called a word processor that would allow text changes and copy making without erasers and carbon paper, it sounded like another impossible dream.

It was 1985, and I was ready to start working on my doctoral dissertation. My supportive and understanding husband bought me a brand new IBM desk computer. It had a memory of only 256K, used 5-inch floppy disks, and sported a black screen with glowing green letters, but it was beautiful. Out went the electric typewriter, in came the computer, and I never looked back. But within the university, and particularly in the English department, I heard discussions about the damage computers were going to do to research. "How will we know what an author really wrote," scholars were asking, "if we can't see the handwritten manuscripts and the changes the author made?"

It was 1991, and I was a full-fledged assistant professor of medieval history at a small liberal arts college. I was excited that year to be helping to sponsor a traveling exhibit of 10th and 11th century manuscripts from the Monastery of St. Gall. A friend and I were co-lecturing in a class on monasticism to go along with the exhibit. A student brought me a cartoon showing several monks standing around a copy machine, with a caption reading, "It's a miracle." The cartoon was an obvious takeoff on the current ad campaign being run by the Xerox company, but I kept it taped to the door of my office until the tape cracked and the edges of the paper curled up and started to flake away. Life seemed to be getting simpler all the time, and fewer and fewer of us were questioning what was being lost in the process. I certainly wasn't.

It was the year 2000—the turn of a century—and people were worried about the consequences of changing from the 19s to the 20s. What would happen to all those printed checkbooks, invoices, order forms, and account statements with a blank space for the date that looked like this: _____, 19___? There was near panic over the possibility that on January 1, 2000, computers would crash and lose all their records because they had not been programed to handle the dates of the 21st century. We adapted, of course, but a bit of nostalgia began to creep in. One contest asked, "What was the most important invention of the past 1000 years?" The run away winner? Gutenberg's printing press, which made books available to ordinary people.

Now it's 2012, and we're witnessing the decline of bookstores, publishers, and paper-based publications of all sorts. Bookstore chains like Borders are closing, newspapers are folding (not meant as a pun!), magazines are shrinking, and electronic editions of books are outselling printed versions by a wide margin. Earlier this year, a friend and fellow blogger asked if it was worth it any longer to publish bound versions of our books. I confess, I don't know. I have a carton of trade paper books sitting here in my closet, while checks from Kindle keep rolling in every month.

I can't claim to have a crystal ball to tell me what the future holds for writers. I don't even know what it holds for me as a writer. But for whatever the voice of experience is worth, this small book will offer some suggestions on finding your way through the thickets of the publishing world. I am only a small mouse among the hordes of new authors, but I've found a little piece of cheese, called an Amazon bestseller ranking, and I'd like to share with you some of the methods I used to get there. The following chapters are, for the most part, culled from the blog posts I've left along the way. I'm happy to scatter the crumbs of my experience and leave a trail that may help you find your own path through the traps that lay ahead.

1. Try Something New

Shortly after my book, *Beyond All Price*, came out, I received this series of questions from a reader:

If I may ask, I'm quite curious to know why you chose self-publishing for your books rather than going the traditional publisher route? There are so many history buffs in the world, I would think there's a huge market for your work, both fiction and non-fiction, and you have the credentials to back you up. Was it to have more control over your work? Did you go through traditional publishers at first and they weren't interested? And, have you had success in self-publishing, volume-wise?

I started by correcting a couple of assumptions. There are many history buffs in the world, I agreed, but that does not mean they make up a huge market for my particular book. I am constantly amazed at how narrowly some people limit their interests. I've been writing about a particular regiment—the 100th Pennsylvania Volunteers. One descendant of a soldier in that regiment sent me a note, saying he probably would not be buying my first Civil War book because most of my characters were in Company C and he was interested in Company K. Fair enough. He's entitled to his own interests.

Next, the writer says I have the credentials to back me up. In some ways I do. I am a trained historian—a retired Professor Emerita at a good and well-known liberal arts college. But my own specialty as a professor was in the history of Anglo-Norman church-state relationships in the twelfth century. How's that for narrow? It says nothing about what qualifications I have to write about the Civil War.

∞◦∞

Learning from Past Mistakes

After I retired from active college teaching, I decided to explore a long-repressed interest in America's Civil War because, for the first time, I was free to do so. Before retirement, I had published two books, but both were controlled by the rules and standard practices of academic presses. I found publishers for both of them because I was fairly well known within the small subset of historians who were working on topics closely related to 12th-century Europe. I was also willing to accept the fact that I would never make a dime from those books.

Academic scholars write books to demonstrate that they belong in the profession. They write because it is a requirement if they want to get a job, and it is an even bigger requirement if they want to earn promotion and tenured status. The first publishing contract I signed guaranteed me fifteen cents per copy of my book—after the first ten thousand copies were sold. Since there aren't that many people in the whole world interested in a monograph about the diplomatic maneuvers of Bishop Arnulf of Lisieux, I knew from the start that I'd never see that fifteen cents. I was content to see the book in print and to know that it was being favorably reviewed by other academics.

Now, let's jump ahead several years. It was 2003 and I was working on a Civil War history called *A Scratch with the Rebels*. It was based at least in part on some letters written by my great uncle. I had a good story to tell, the facts to flesh it out, and all that history training behind me. After I had written a few chapters, I applied for an NEH grant, hoping to finance my research trips to South Carolina. I didn't get it, but one of the judges was sufficiently impressed to tell an editor at a university press in the state where my regiment had been recruited. She was taken by the proposal, sent the chapters off to readers, and came back with the advice to make sure I was writing for a general audience and to concentrate on telling the story. I finished writing the manuscript while I waited for a contract to arrive. My editor left for a better job without warning. Her managing editor took over the project, put it on a back burner, and left it there for ten months. Then she informed me they were no longer interested.

Undaunted, I shipped it off to another university press where I had a contact, and at first the new editor was enthusiastic. He sent it off to be read by several Civil War experts (and I should have known right then that I was doomed.) Eventually the readers' comments came back, and they all had to do with things like how much of the book needed to be more theoretical, how I had failed to discuss all the relevant research that was going on in the field, and that too much of the book was based on personal letters—a story—rather than "historical records." My new editor really tried, I think, to explain to my critics that I was writing a book for a general audience, not for an academic search committee, but in the end it didn't matter. I had no reputation as a Civil War historian, and the field was simply not open to newcomers. The editor retired, and the dog-eared and well-traveled manuscript came back to me.

It had been over three years by then, and I was discouraged. An e-mail from that first editor urged me to persevere. She recommended a small private press that specialized in Pennsylvania history and the Civil War. Not bothering this time with a formal query letter, I called them. They asked for an e-mailed copy of the manuscript, and six days later, I had a contract in hand. Success?

Not really! The press was easy to work with, and the royalties were three times what I would have received from a university press. There were drawbacks, however. I had no control over the layout or appearance of the book, which came out looking entirely too much like a high school textbook. Quality problems existed, too—the plastic coating on the cover began to peel almost immediately, and all the press offered was a suggestion that I use a warm iron to reseal the coating before I tried to sell my copies. No one had ever warned me that I might be expected to iron my books!

The press also turned out to have little knowledge or experience in marketing and distribution. They featured *A Scratch with the Rebels* in their catalog, but it only appeared a couple of times a year and was limited to people who had purchased other books from them. Their chosen distributing company failed to put the books out on display and simply returned them after a few months. In the end, the press sold only a few books, and my total royalties amounted to about $25.00. The only copies that did sell were those I bought myself at half-price and resold to my friends and at a couple of book signings.

By the beginning of 2009, I had devoted six years to *A Scratch with the Rebels*—with almost nothing to show for it. I had made some major mistakes along the way, I admit, but I also had learned that the publishing market for the average writer was a field full of mousetraps for the unwary. By then I was working on a new book—my first historical novel, *Beyond All Price*. I knew I needed to find a new approach.

☙❧

Testing the Marketing Waters

Once I started working seriously on my Civil War novel, *Beyond All Price*, I also began looking for ways to publish it. Waiting until you have a finished product just does not work; you have to do your homework along the way. I started with the standard approaches. I found books written in my genre (in this case historical fiction set in 1860s) and checked on their publishers and the authors' agents. These were names I could at least be sure would be open to the type of book I was writing. To that basic list, I added other publishing houses and literary agents I found listed in such resources as *Writer's Market*. I looked up each one on the Internet to find out how they wanted submissions handled. Each one on the list received a hand-tailored written or e-mailed query letter.

Responses were spotty. Almost half never replied. Others sent canned messages: "Sorry. We are not accepting new clients." "Sorry. We no longer consider unsolicited manuscripts." Only a handful expressed any interest whatsoever, and they consistently asked for a full description of my platform before they would consider the book. At that stage, I had no idea what a "platform" looked like in the publishing world, so I had more research ahead of me.

Here's what I found. If you are a household word—a politician, a celebrity, a sports figure, or a best-selling author already—you have a built-in platform: a fan base of people who will buy your book because of who you are. If you're a hard-working writer, you have to build your own platform. Publishers and agents suggested that I needed the following:

- A personal website visited by hundreds of readers every day;
- A blog that had a similar reader base and gathered dozens of comments on every posting;
- A personal Facebook page, with hundreds of followers and daily postings;
- A Facebook Fan Page, one dedicated to my writing;
- A Twitter account, with daily postings and thousands of followers;
- A LinkedIn account, with multiple recommendations and connections within my professional community;
- A personal e-mail list of media outlets, bookstores, libraries, and civic organizations, all of which would be eager to do personal interviews with me, invite me as a guest speaker, or host a book-signing event.

Fortunately, I'm pretty adept at finding my way around a computer, but I had never bothered to become involved in social networking of this sort. I went to work, particularly at building my Internet resources. These outlets are not hard to use, but they take an enormous amount of time to develop their full potential. I've been working on this platform for about eighteen months now, and my numbers surprise me. I have almost 400 Facebook friends, some 800 Twitter followers, more than 290 connections on LinkedIn, and a website/blog that receives around 200 hits a day. To me, that's amazing, but the figures are still not up to the five thousand guaranteed readers that most publishers want to see. At most, I have a little soapbox that serves as my platform.

One other factor weighed into my publishing quandary. That year—2011—marked the beginning of a five-year commemoration of the Civil War. Right now, interest in Civil War history is at an all-time high, and I expect enthusiasm to last for most of the next five years. But by 2016, we're all going to be tired of the topic. My window of opportunity is right here and now. If I wanted *Beyond All Price* to benefit from the increased coverage of the Civil War, it had to be ready to go. I simply did not have time to spend several more years pursuing followers, then agents, and then publishers. There seemed to be only one other path to putting the book into the hands of willing readers—self-publishing.

❧

Making the First Decisions

As I negotiated the paths of writing and publishing for a general audience rather than an academic one, I learned a lot. I knew I could no longer rely on a professional identity to pave my way, and that I had only made a start at building a viable platform as an author. I recognized the warning signs as publishers reacted to a faltering economy by restricting their publications to authors they could count on to generate huge sales. And I had identified my niche among potential readers.

My real breakthrough, however, came as a result of some random questions from a casual acquaintance. "I'm betting that you write exactly the kinds of books you most enjoy reading," he said. "So how do you choose? When you walk into a bookstore, do you browse or head straight to pick up what you want? Do you buy best sellers or look for hidden gems? Do you buy hardbacks or paperbacks? Do you want a quick read, or a hefty volume to fill long hours? What kind of cover makes you pick up a book and examine it? If you know what kind of book you buy, you'll understand what your readers want from you."

His point was well taken, but my answers brought me up short. You see, I am a dedicated Kindle owner. Gadgets fascinate me, and I'm frequently the first to adopt new technology. I bought my Kindle in 2008, and since then my book purchases have dwindled to a trickle. I've purchased a couple of used editions of books that are out of print, but I don't buy new books unless I can get them in an electronic edition.

That surprises even me. I was intrigued by the idea of a Kindle. But I've always loved the feel and heft and smell of books. They fill my office, every end table, and overflow the living room book case. I thought reading on a Kindle would be a novelty, but I didn't expect the device to become transparent, leaving only me and the printed word—just the way a book does. I found the Kindle much easier to carry around than a stack of books, and my hands didn't get tired holding a heavy book. The cat quit stealing my bookmarks because they no longer dangled out of the book.

I knew I had come to depend on my Kindle in ways I never expected. Kindle provides immediate and inexpensive gratification. If I hear about a book I want to read, I can buy it and start reading in less than a minute. I upload research documents that I want to have instantly available. I now have an application that allows me to read Kindle texts on my desk computer, my iPhone, or my iPad. All those devices sync themselves, so that I never lose my place or misplace a text when I move from one device to another. What kind of a book do I choose for myself? Obviously, the answer is one that comes in an electronic version.

And there was the answer to all my publishing dilemmas. Kindle editions (and the other versions that are now coming out) don't require a traditional publisher. In fact, in some cases, having a traditional publishing contract limits or squelches an author's ability to jump into the e-book market. I learned how serious that problem is when I tried to talk the publisher of *A Scratch with the Rebels* into doing a Kindle edition. Eventually they tried, but they did a really poor job of it and refused to advertise that the e-book was available because it cut into their profits.

I was about to become a self-published author. I have to admit that the idea made me slightly uncomfortable in the beginning, because I was still carrying around some leftover baggage from my days as an academic. Most professors have run into one or two folks who use a vanity press to publish their books because no one else will touch them. Within the university, publishing with a vanity press—in effect paying somebody to publish your book— was a career killer. My first hurdle was recognizing the difference between a vanity press (which charges a hefty sum to produce a book) and a self-publishing company (which allows an author to contract for services only when production assistance is necessary).

My production company of choice was CreateSpace, a subsidiary of Amazon. If they accept a book for publication, they do not charge for the privilege. They will provide guidance on how to prepare a manuscript for Kindle, and they will carry the Kindle edition in the Amazon catalog. The author pays nothing up front; the company takes a small cut of any sales for its handling and delivery of the e-book. They offer more elaborate services, of course. I wanted my *Beyond All Price* to be available in trade paper, so I contracted for their printing services. That also meant that they would sell my books on Amazon, thus releasing me from the need to distribute all my books myself. Because I wanted the book to look as professional as possible, I also paid a layout person to handle things like interior appearance, margins, and pagination. Those were services I could not do myself.

Traditional publishers, of course, do more than print a book, but I felt fairly confident of my ability to provide those other services. I already knew exactly how I wanted my cover to look, and I owned the photograph I wanted to use. All I had to do was prepare the cover art and submit it to the printer. All manuscripts need editing; traditional publishers have their own editors to proofread, catch stupid errors, and clean up grammar and punctuation. In my case, I had years of editing experience of my own, and a couple of talented friends who were willing to comb through the manuscript to catch any errors I missed. I did not think I needed to pay an editor. Publishers also assume some responsibility for marketing a book, although in recent years they have demanded that authors do more and more of their own marketing. Since I already had an Internet presence, as well as a small but loyal base of followers, and since I was writing for an electronic audience, it was easy to do my own marketing.

Was it the right decision? So far, I have to believe it was. In the current market, bookstores are closing and e-book sales are leaping ahead. Within the first three months, I had sold more copies of *Beyond All Price* on Amazon and Kindle than the total three-year sales of my last traditionally published book. Plus, Kindle pays 70% royalties, while my traditional publishing contracts offered 5% to 12%. Oh, I'm not going to get rich from the sales I generate. But I have paid off all my publishing costs, and I am in complete control of future sales. I'm my own publisher, and I love it.

2. View Publishing As A Business

Forming your own publishing company will make you feel important and make you rich! (Well, maybe not the rich part, but it is an ego boost.) More important, if you don't have your own company imprint, like mine, Katzenhaus Books, your books will carry the name of the production company you use. Not a good idea, especially when most readers do not understand the difference between a print-on-demand company and a vanity press. Starting your own business is just a matter of doing it. You don't even have to file papers on it formally until it is making a profit of several thousand dollars. And in the meantime, while you are waiting for your book sales to make you rich, you can at least take your expenses off your income tax if you are the sole proprietor of a small business. What's not to love? Here's how to go about it.

❧

Formulating a Business Plan

It's one thing to decide you'll self-publish your new book. It's another to take all the steps necessary to become a publisher. Here's the point you must understand: publishing a book starts long before the book is written. Publishing is a business, not an afterthought. Establishing a business was my first step.

A business needs a definition and a name. I started with the name, something I could use as a publishing imprint on my books. I didn't want anything that would identify me too closely—not my name or a street address, nothing too cutesy, but something that would lend itself to a neat little logo. After coming up with several ideas, only to discover by way of a Google search that the name was already being used, I looked around the room where I was sitting and realized that all four of my cats were there keeping me company. My first thought was, "This is like living in a cat house." Then, realizing the unfortunate connotations of that word, I switched to German, coming up with Katzenhaus Books and a simple black cat silhouette as a logo.

Next I asked myself what I wanted this business to do. The answer was fairly straightforward. Katzenhaus Books would produce, publish, promote, and sell one or more books of original historical fiction. It would remain flexible enough to expand into other book types. Perhaps eventually it would be able to offer similar services or advice to other writers who were seeking independent publishing choices.

Any business needs capital and a financial plan. During my academic career, I had relied on research grants to support the writing process, a publishing contract to pay production costs, and a publisher to bear the burdens of advertising and distribution. All I had to do was write. Now, all those expenses came back to me. I started my financial analysis by comparing several years of our living expenses against our income to discover how much discretionary income I had to play with. After deciding how much I could afford to risk on this venture, I did some research on self- publishing companies to estimate the total cost of a typical book. What I discovered was a wide range of prices, depending on how much help I was going to need.

The next step involved an honest examination of my own knowledge and abilities. I had easy access to most of the research materials I would be using, so I would not need to do a whole lot of initial travel. I'm a professional historian, a pretty good writer, and an experienced copy editor. Writing was not going to be a problem. Advertising and distribution remained question marks, but I had some experience in doing book signings and conference presentations. I was also an experienced webmaster. When it comes to book design, on the other hand, I'm pretty much out of my element. While I might have an idea or two about how I wanted a particular book to look, I was going to need someone to do the actual cover and interior layout. It appeared that I could afford to pay for some contracted design services and handle production costs out of the nest egg I had identified. Then I worked on establishing a book price that would make it possible to re-coup my expenditures.

My private resolve was to produce the book I was eager to write within the next two years. I needed to sell enough copies first to restore the savings account and then to accumulate enough of a cushion to finance any future book. I gave myself an estimated eighteen months to two years to accomplish that. If, at the end of four years, I had not made a profit, I decided I would retire from the publishing business and take up knitting or crossword puzzles.

⁓

The Home Office

Establishing your own business has tax advantages. Once you have a plan and a named business, you can declare it as a "sole proprietorship" on your income tax and start taking deductions for all those expenses. The biggest deduction will come from establishing your home office as your principle, regular, and exclusive place of business. What does that mean? Well, basically, no more writing at one end of the dining room table and then shoving the papers out of the way to serve dinner. You must have a clearly defined space in which you conduct all the activities associated with your business—writing, researching, editing, advertising, shipping. It does not have to be a large space. You can fit an office into a large closet, in a cubbyhole under the stairs, in the basement or the attic, or into a section of a room that is clearly separated from all other activities there. It simply must be used for your business and for nothing else. You'll need a desk, a filing cabinet, and—most important—a place to keep everything separate from the other parts of your life.

I was fortunate to have my own space already designated. When we moved into our new condo, we had the builders convert what started out as an open den area into a third "bedroom" with a small closet. My husband had already claimed a smaller room as his place to work on all his Lions Club business. This new room was to be mine. It has evolved into a cozy hideaway that makes a perfect home office. My initial requirements were these: a door that closed, lots of natural light, phone and computer cable connections, and a few creature comforts. I furnished it first with bookcases and a large slab table to serve as a computer desk. And here's what it holds at the moment. I've added risers at the back of the desk slab to lift frequently used office supplies, the printer, the cable modem, the backup drive, and other components off the main desk. Two low filing cabinets flank the desk to hold research files and other supplies while providing additional space to stack stuff. The closet is now full of industrial shelving to hold overflows of books, files, shipping supplies, and extra computer elements. An upholstered rocking chair and a floor lamp positioned between the accordion folding doors of the closet provide a hidden reading nook. A futon, full of pillows and a fuzzy throw, waits for the moment when I really need a quick nap.

The atmosphere is welcoming. The walls are painted a bright, energetic tangerine. A magnetic white board allows me to leave notes or pin up interesting pictures or publicity clippings. The large picture window opens onto a grove of cedars and cypress trees. The rocking chair sits on its own little oriental rug, and a tiffany lamp gently lights my desk area. On the walls are some award plaques, my diplomas, and a huge etching of St. John's College, Oxford, where I was lucky enough to teach for three separate summers. Scattered around the room are a few stuffed animals from special places—a bear from Gettysburg dressed as a Union soldier, another bear dressed as one of the guards from Buckingham palace, the ragged little puppy from Poogan's Porch in Charleston, and the stately lion from the Biltmore estate.

Finally, there are the reminders of the purpose of this particular office. Sitting on the frame above the entry door is a cutout of a black cat, looking exactly like the Katzenhaus cat from my business cards. A brass Civil War cannon acts as a paperweight. The closet door sports a street sign that says "Frogmore" in honor of an upcoming book. (And no, I didn't steal it; I bought it in a souvenir shop on St. Helena Island.) My favorite piece is a replica of a Civil War era rag doll. It is reversible; at one end is a black slave "Momma" wearing an apron and a turban. Turn her over, and you reveal a red-haired white woman. The storyboard says that a slave woman made the doll for the small child she tended. When the white "Massa" appeared, the doll could be quickly reversed to look like the child's real mother—and then reversed again for the more beloved Momma. To me it serves as a reminder of the two different perspectives—the slave and the white missionary—that fill my new book.

The result is eclectic, but definitely my principle, regular, and exclusive place of business. When I'm here, I'm working. Even the cats have learned to respect the boundary of the doorway. They will wander in once in a while, but only to curl up quietly on the floor or the futon, thus keeping it Katzenhaus in fact as well as spirit.

ღალ

Tax Deductions for Writers

The Internal Revenue Service has a soft spot for writers. Who would have guessed! Once you admit that you are an author by claiming that designation as your profession, the tax laws are on your side. Someone in Washington actually understands that book production takes a long time, and that you can work at it for years without making any profit, because you are still creating the book, not selling it. They will grant your deductions for expenses for up to five years before they start refusing your claims to be a "real" writer. On your tax return, don't list yourself as "store clerk" or "plumber's assistant" while you are writing. There's a special designation for writers. Find it and use it. Oh, you should keep your day job, but think of yourself as a writer and regard "fry cook" as your hobby, not the other way around. Then start collecting your deductions.

Have you set up your home office? Then you have a place of business. Measure the space in square feet, determine the square footage of your entire house or apartment, and then figure out the percentage of the residence that is exclusively used for business. (A 10 x 12 office in a 1500 square-foot house = 8% devoted to business use.) That percentage now applies to all of your housing expenses that affect the entire space—heating and lighting bills, rent or mortgage interest, insurance, homeowner association fees, security system, and termite protection are all common expenses. You can't deduct painting the living room if you use the back bedroom as your office, but you can deduct 8% of the cost of a new roof, since that applies to the entire structure, and 8% of the roof covers your office.

Next, take a look at your home office and its contents. If you are using an old card table and a folding chair for a desk, you probably can't deduct their cost, but if you go out and purchase a new computer desk, using it only for your writing, its price will be deductible. New or fairly recent electronics (computer, printer, external backup drive) can be deducted or depreciated. The first phone line into your residence is not deductible, but if you add a second line for a fax machine or an 800 number for your business, you've found another deduction.

Be sure to keep track of all expenses for office supplies— pens, pencils, notepads, printer cartridges, diskettes, scotch tape, paper clips, file folders, labels, a calendar, an appointment book, scissors, a rack to hold current file folders. You can even deduct the cost of air, if you buy it in compressed form and use it to clean your keyboard. (I use mine to chase the cat off the desk, but the principle is the same.)

Think advertising. Anything you have printed with the name of your company or the name of your next book can be deducted as an advertising expense. Of course you'll have a supply of business cards, but you can also use the same size card to announce an upcoming book. (I had some printed with a picture of "The Second Mouse" on them. I have a second set of half-size business cards with photographs of Beaufort, SC, on them to advertise my next novel, *The Road to Frogmore*.) Both were deductible, as are bookmarks that match your book covers or brochures telling dealers and bookstores how they can order your books.

Much of your book budget will go for travel—to research libraries, book signings, or writing conferences. If you travel by car, you can deduct the exact mileage, as long as you keep a log or record of the odometer. You'll be asked for details of the car's purchase price, its year and model, its VIN, and its total mileage, so keep them handy. You'll be able to deduct 50 to 55 cents a mile if your travel is purely for business. I bought a magnetic company sign for under $10.00. On business trips, I slap that on the front door of the family sedan and turn the entire trip into a business expense. You can also deduct hotel bills, parking fees, and bridge or road tolls if you keep records.

And finally, you'll need to keep careful count of the books you order for resale. With a print-on-demand contract, you don't have to keep a huge inventory on hand, but you'll need a constant supply of printed books to give away, to send to book reviewers, to sell to your friends, to take with you to speaking engagements, or to enter into book contests. You may be asked to report your sales and to pay sales tax, so you'll need to account for every copy you purchase. Be sure to check with your municipal and state laws on sales tax. In my state, you don't have to report sales for tax purposes until your sales go over $3000.00, but that may not be true for where you live. The books you sell will cost you a bit, but the ones you give away can be deducted.

For many authors, these expenses can mount up to a tax deduction of several thousand dollars. Just remember that you are expected to be earning a profit after five years of effort. If you are making money, you can only deduct expenses that exceed your income. If you are not making any money after five years, the IRS will tell you that writing is now your hobby and deny any deductions. It will be time to declare your real occupation as fry cook or plumber's helper.

∽✐∾

Assembling a Staff

Self-publishing is something of a misnomer. The process of taking a book from first idea to a spot on someone's bookshelf requires the help and talents of many people. The work used to be done by huge publishing houses. When you decide to self-publish, the responsibility for all the many tasks involved falls squarely on your shoulders. You are already the author, the editor-in-chief, and the business owner. You cannot hope to sit isolated in your little home office and do everything yourself, no matter how talented you may be. The success of your book will depend upon how well you assemble a team of assistants. Here's a look at the staff I have assembled. Perhaps it will give you some ideas.

My most important hire was my husband. Of course he was already on board to give me moral support, but as time went on, he took upon himself three important roles. First, he is my travel agent. Once I decide on the need for a research trip or agree to do a talk, a book signing, or a conference appearance, he takes over. He plans the itinerary, books our accommodations, and provides the transportation. Second, he is my mail clerk. He's much better than I at packing and wrapping, and he never seems to mind a quick trip to the post office. I can count on him to mail single book purchases or handle large book shipments. And third, he is my official photographer. Whether I need a special shot for an illustration or some general pictures to help me set a scene, he is there with his camera. You can see a sample of his work on the cover of *Beyond All Price*. He also comes with the advantage of being inexpensive. His salary is $1.00 a year, augmented by clean laundry, home-cooked meals, and endless affection and gratitude.

My business plan recognized that I would need to hire a design artist to create the book cover and a layout expert to make sure that the final book meets the exacting standards of the publishing world—page numbers, attractive fonts, spacing, chapter titles, and flourishes all in place. Since both those areas are way beyond my expertise, I hired both functions through the production company who contracted to produce the physical book.

I found another source of staff members at a company called Vistaprint. I got started there by ordering my first business cards for Katzanhaus Books. From that one order, I learned about their other great promotional items and ended up buying a magnetic sign for the side of the car, postcards, brochures, a tote bag, and several other items with my own logos on them. Then I found that they also provided hosting for websites and blogs, as well as domain names and e-mail addresses for companies. I was able to use their services for all my promotional and web-based needs.

You will need a banker. Money is important, but many people are not trained to handle it efficiently. I certainly wasn't. My first lesson came when a friend of a friend bought a book from me and handled me a check. When I looked at it the next day, I found that she had made it out to Katzenhaus Books. I took it to the bank, only to have it rejected. I couldn't cash it because I didn't have an account in the name of Katzenhaus Books. I could either hunt down the person and ask for another check (embarrassing!) or open a business account as Carolyn Schriber, DBA (doing business as) Katzenhaus Books. Since there was a real possibility that other checks would follow the same pattern, I went ahead and opened the account. A good move, as it turned out, since the account came with an associated credit card that lets me keep business purchases separated from household purchases. It also provided safe direct deposits for royalty payments.

At about the same time, I realized that I needed to be able to take book orders on my website, which in turn meant I needed to have a credit card manager. Despite what you may have heard, most people trust PayPal to handle their credit card purchases. The service they provide is the easiest—and the safest—way to handle such charges. I've never had a PayPal charge that was not paid in full, and the company is good about forwarding customer information. They charge only a couple of percentage points on each transaction, and those are pennies well spent in terms of convenience. Granted, occasionally I get a "phishing" attack on my account, asking that I send in my bank account number, but since all such requests are by definition fraudulent, there is no real danger of an account being compromised. Further, PayPal is good about tracking down the perpetrators if you send them copies of any such e-mails. I use their services constantly without problems.

To extend my outreach, I needed the help of professional promoters. I found my greatest help came from three sources. First, the wonderful reading site, BookBuzzr, not only created a free on-screen reader for each of my books, but also continues to offer me clever new ways to advertise the books for free. I gained access to professional trade shows by subscribing to NABE, the North American Booksellers Exchange. The connections I have made through professional writers' organizations have also been invaluable. Writers are tremendously generous folks, probably because we've all been in the same trenches fighting the same wars.

When *Beyond All Price* began to make a lot of money—not a fortune, but more than I ever expected—I sought more help with money management. A financial advisor helped clarify the best uses for unexpected windfalls. He found flexible investment ideas that helped preserve the principle while providing a way to start earning interest on the money. He also introduced me to an absolute necessity—an accountant who could help me organize my records and deal with the tax complications that come with self-employment taxes and irregular income schedules.

Somewhere along the line, I received an e-mail from a would-be film maker, asking whether I had protected my film rights to the book and if they were for sale. At that point, I had no idea. But I quickly learned that I needed the advice of an intellectual property lawyer to guide me through the intricacies of formal copyright registration and to prepare a simple options contract that would guard against anyone snatching my story and profiting from turning it into a movie without my knowledge.

I relied on friends for many things. They served as sounding boards when I needed to talk through an idea. They volunteered as pre-publication manuscript readers to check for unfortunate typos, blatant errors, and unintentional omissions. They were my first salesmen as they talked about the book to their other friends, and, throughout the process, they were faithful cheerleaders. A couple of them are still reposting my blogs and tweets to keep spreading the word. I couldn't have done it without them.

So there are the people I needed in order to "self-publish" a single book. Even I am surprised at how many there are: travel agent, mail clerk, photographer, design artist, layout expert, production company, printer, web host, banker, credit card manager, professional promoters, financial advisor, accountant, lawyer, sounding boards, manuscript readers, salesmen, and cheerleaders. Each of them deserves partial credit for any success my book has achieved. If you're beginning this same process, start now to identify the staff that can help you along the way.

❧

Obtaining Your ISBN

If you want to sell your book in any retail outlet, whether it is a book chain, an independent shop, or an online source such as Amazon, or if you want your book in any library, it must have an International Standard Book Number (ISBN). Every country has a single agency responsible for issuing ISBNs. In the United States, the company is Bowker Identifier Services.

Publishers—including self-publishers—may register their company and contact information with Bowker and order anywhere from one to one thousand ISBNs. Then when a specific number is assigned to a particular book, the publisher goes to the Bowker website and registers the number and title. That guarantees that purchasers will be able to find your book, and that the book will be listed in *Books In Print*, among other bibliographic resources. Don't skip this step. The lack of an ISBN number marks the book and its author as rank amateurs.

Every book should have a number, and each number can be used only once. A new edition, or a different format, will require a new number. Originally ISBNs had ten digits. In 1998, the numbers were expanded to a thirteen-digit format, with the first three digits being 978. That will remain the case for the foreseeable future, but it provides for the possibility of change if all available numbers are exhausted. The numbers are broken into five parts of variable length. The first three are always 978. The second section represents the country; the third, the publisher; the fourth, the title, and the fifth, a code number that can be used to verify the other sections.

Most printing/publishing companies will offer to provide your book with its own ISBN, but that means that the book will be listed with the imprint of the production company: for example, Smashwords, or CreateSpace, or Lightning Source will appear as the publisher of record. If you want your own publishing company listed, you must purchase your ISBN directly from Bowker.

I had already decided that I want to publish under my own imprint, "Katzenhaus Books," not the book production company, and that meant I had to procure my own ISBN number. Next decision: they sell one number for $125.00 or ten for $250.00. It's a bargain, right? But at the end of months of writing, I had reached the "never again stage" and wasn't at all sure I would ever need more than one. After agonizing a bit, I opted to order ten, all the time feeling ridiculously extravagant.

Then I started checking on other matters. While I love print books and definitely want my book to be an object people can pick up and examine, I also love my Kindle. And I'm hopelessly infatuated with the new iPad. I wanted my book available in all available formats.

So what difference did that make? Well, you don't have to have an ISBN for the Kindle edition, but you can provide one, and it's useful if you plan to issue in several formats. And if you plan to publish an Apple version? You have to go through Smashwords, a company that formats your manuscript for all other e-book platforms (Sony, B&N, Palm, etc.). Smashwords requires an ISBN that is different from both the print version and the Kindle version. I already needed three ISBNs for my single book. I actually saved myself $125.00 by ordering the set of ten.

Many bookstores require books to have a printed barcode—also issued by Bowker. The barcode is a graphical representation of the book's ISBN and its retail price. That decision is up to you, and it may be that your local bookstore will accept the book without a barcode. However, they are relatively inexpensive, and they give the book that final published look.

∾ා౿ා

Copyright Law

Now, a brief word on copyright. The law does not require authors to pay for (or even register) their copyrights. Full copyright protection comes automatically when you write anything. Don't let anyone charge you for that copyright. Just make sure your manuscript has that all-important symbol: Copyright © Year of Publication and Your Name. It goes on the second page, the reverse of your title. That's it. That's all you really have to do.

It is possible, however, to register your copyright with the Library of Congress. Having the copyright registered provides an additional degree of protection if your book should ever end up in a court of law. For example, if someone plagiarizes your work and passes it off as his own, it may help to be able to point to the date on which you registered the copyright. You'll have to decide for yourself if the registration fees are worth it.

I didn't think it was, until my book started to gain national attention and the first screenwriter came sniffing around my copyright set-up. Then I learned that $35.00 was a cheap safeguard, particularly when I compared it to what a successful screen version of the book might earn. It is now possible to file your registration online and mail in two copies of the book to complete the process. I say, do it.

You will definitely want to obtain a Library of Congress cataloging number, which guarantees that your book will be included in the Library of Congress catalog for all time. Librarians also want to see an LCCN to tell them how to enter the book into their own cataloguing system. The publisher must send the first copy of the completed book to the Library of Congress, where someone will record all the necessary data describing the book and create an original catalog entry. Your production company should take care of that for you, although they may charge you a fee. Then the production company adds the assigned number to all copies of the book.

3. Build An Online Platform

Your online platform consists of all the contacts you can make with people who might be interested in buying your book and reading your content. The Internet has made it possible to reach out to audiences all over the world. Now you need to start establishing your presence and meeting your potential audiences.

Start exploring the advice available on the Internet, keeping in mind that not all sources are equally valuable. If I had to choose one marketing tool, it would be BookBuzzr. Their variety of services gives you much to choose from. Be sure to get your book widget, which lets you put your whole book in an inch of space almost anywhere on the web. If I had to choose one blogger's advice, I'd go to Dana Lynn Smith's Savvy Book Marketer site. For general money-saving tips, you can't go wrong using Carolyn Howard-Johnson's series of "Frugal" web publications.

For the rest, you can find dozens of bloggers and columnists who have made successful careers out of telling others how to use the resources of the Internet. I decided not to recommend any one over the others, because much depends on your own needs and personality. I subscribed to one promising blog, only to discover that the writer knew less than I did about the Internet and could provide only the most basic bits of advice. Another site turned out to be written so far above me that I felt I was reading a foreign language. My best advice is to sample widely and find a few resources that prove helpful.

A word of caution about the usual social media sites may be necessary here. Readers turn to Twitter for pithy sayings, not to be told to "Go buy my book." Facebook provides enough ads as it is. Don't make it worse by using your status updates as another ad. Your readers are probably interested in your signings, your awards, your public speeches—but don't beat them over the head with flat demands for their money. YouTube videos can reach huge audiences, but don't post something unless it makes you look like a professional, not a silly amateur turned loose for the first time with a cellphone. And LinkedIn audiences are even tougher. The participants there are usually serious business people. Give them information they can use, not blatant self-promotion.

The rest is up to you.

❧

Creating Your Website

Once you have decided to create a website (an author page, a book page, or a company page), you'll have to make several important decisions. First, you need a domain name and a web host, somewhere to post your page. The possibilities are endless. Almost everyone has some kind of server these days, and it's hard to know what will be the best deal in your area. Here are a few suggestions and some things to look out for.

First, claim your domain name by registering it with one of several companies that handle these matters. Godaddy.com may be the best known of these, but you can also use Register.com, NetworkSolutions.com, or WebsitePalace.com. They all provide the same services, so check carefully to see what each one charges.

You'll want to find a domain name that is short, simple, and relevant to the purpose of your page. Are you creating an author page? Then use your own name. A book page? Use the title or an abbreviated form of it. A company page? Then you'll want the name of the company. (Avoid initials or acronyms unless you're as well known as IBM or AT&T). You may also want to register the same term with several different extensions. You don't want anyone to leap onto your reputation and steal your name for another site. Don't just register SamSmith.com; you also should own SamSmith.org, SamSmith.net, SamSmith.biz.

Now you must choose a web host, and it is up to you to decide whether you want a free one or one that charges a monthly fee. Sound like a no-brainer? It's not. Free sites are widely available. Some of the best known and most popular are on Google, or companies like Blogger.com or Yola.com. Your decision depends on the purpose of the site. At the moment, I have a free website on Blogger, where I can post some of the outtakes from books I'm writing. They are there because I love them, but they don't fit into the book. I'm offering them for free to my dedicated followers, who want something new to read.

The site works because it suits my purpose, but it has several drawbacks. The URL is onthroadtofrogmore.blogspot.com. The inclusion of "blogspot.com" in the URL tells everyone that this is a free site, and really savvy Internet users—and most search engines—will automatically reject it as not a "serious" site. I also do not have complete control of the content. I can't transfer the articles easily, and Blogger could shut me down at any moment. I can't run ads, or sell anything on the page, although pop-up ads not of my choosing may appear.

For my more serious site, the one that supports my independent publishing company and its publications, I use a paid site hosted by Vistaprint. This is a personal choice, and a relatively little-known one. Vistaprint also handles many of my printing needs, such as business cards, banners, brochures and items with my company logo, which means that my website can use the same graphics and "match" my other advertising items. I can use my own domain name—KatzenhausBooks.com—and use the pages as I wish, to carry an order form for my books or to open it to other advertising. So far, I have been well satisfied.

Other popular choices include Bluehost, Drupal, Wordpress, Dreamweaver, Powweb, Site Build it, or HostGator. Their options and learning curves vary greatly, and I recommend you survey them carefully before jumping to any one. Perhaps the best way to choose is to look at websites you really like, and then consult with their owners to find out what host and software they are using. Take advantage of those who have gone before you. You really don't have to re-invent the wheel to create a website. It can be as easy or as complicated as you wish.

$\infty \mathcal{C} \infty$

Designing Your Webpage

I've been designing webpages since 1995, so I've seen a lot of new ideas come and go. Web pages are somewhat akin to fashion. What makes a page look bright and modern one day will stigmatize it as old-fashioned a week later. No one finds a plain white page with small black type attractive, but add one too many colors or pictures and you have a page people will hate because it's too "busy." Where is the line between boring and gaudy, between childish and hopelessly complicated? Here are a few tips I've picked up along the way.

Your page must reflect the subject matter it contains. You can't sell cheese on a flower-strewn background, and it takes a clever florist to work a skunk into an ad for roses. (Actually, I've seen that one, but the florist's name was "Pugh.") When I was running ORB, the "Online Source Book for Medieval History", my page designer came up with a lovely medieval scene for our headline banner. This book, *The Second Mouse Gets the Cheese*, uses a cartoon mouse throughout the chapter headings, so the title of the book's webpage appears in a cartoon font. There's great room for error, however. Littering the page with too many medieval objects or too many mice will eventually irritate your viewers. I recommend picking one element to show the theme, and then letting the page's information carry the theme from then on.

Flash introductions used to be popular, as did animated gifs, which had little characters running across the computer screen. They are no longer surprising. Now they delay the appearance of the real information, and impatient readers will move on. The same is true of sound clips. I considered using a "cheer" on the web page for the online book launch I ran last year. Then a reviewer took me to task. She tried to visit the page at night while other family members were asleep. She was not amused to open the page and be greeted by a raucous crowd.

Other types of animations cause serious problems for viewers with physical limitations. Flashing lights, waving flags, or other sudden or rhythmic visuals may actually trigger seizures in those who are susceptible to such stimuli. Those who are colorblind will miss parts of your page if the contrast between print and background is not great enough. Keystrokes that require two hands may be impossible for some. Information conveyed only by sight will be lost to those who are blind. Illustrations always need to be labeled with tags for those who use software such as "Jaws" to read what appears on the screen.

The quickest way to learn how to design your own webpage is by visiting the pages of others. See what appeals to you and what doesn't. Note that too much information is a turn-off. Pay attention to the ease with which you can navigate the site. Are the buttons or links clearly marked and in a logical spot, or did you have to hunt for them? Was the most important information available quickly, or did you get lost trying to find what you needed? Design your own page to make it easy to use.

For a book or author page, the most important elements should appear at the start—a cover shot and a professional photo of the author (not a snapshot of you at your senior prom.) Contact information is also vital. Today's readers want to know the person behind the book. They want to be able to follow you on Twitter, to connect on Facebook or LinkedIn, to send you an e-mail. I don't recommend ever giving out your home address or phone number; I use a post office box for the address of my publishing company. But it's vital to let your readers feel that you are a real person, one with whom they can communicate.

What else do your potential customers want to find? They want to know a bit about your book—why you wrote it, who your characters are, where and when it takes place, what crisis or problem the main character faces. Tempt them with enough information to spark interest; don't give away the ending.

Customers want to feel important. I try to include a few outtakes from my writing—extra descriptions that only the webpage readers will see. I also use photographs. When I first put up the pages for *Beyond All Price*, I included actual photographs of the real military figures in the story, as well as some 1860s shots of the locations in which the story took place. While I'm still working on *The Road to Frogmore*, I've posted some "then and now" shots of Beaufort, SC, and St. Helena Island. Only faithful blog-readers get to see them.

If you plan to do book-signings or public speaking engagements or radio interviews, be sure to post your schedule. Even if your readers can't attend of these events, they'll feel connected to it. Customers also take vicarious pleasure from any awards you receive; be sure to brag a little when one comes your way. Post a picture of your medal or the fancy sticker on your book. Has your book been reviewed favorably? Post a copy that will tempt potential readers to buy the book. Consider including a formal press release, in case the visitor to your site is a newspaper editor, or the alumni director of your old school, or your local librarian.

Finally, make it easy for the web visitor to order your book. Set up a PayPal account and take orders right from your own website. Or provide good links to your book's sales page on Amazon or other retail source. Your website should make every visitor feel welcome, and it should offer enough variety to invite a second visit. Think of it as your place of business, and let it reflect the best of you.

৩৩৩

How Bloggers Get Started

The best way I know to start a blog is to start. My first efforts were sincerely uninteresting, but I kept at it until I started getting some comments that let me know what my readers were interested in. In my case, they wanted to know how and why I chose self-publishing after several books with established publishers. Once I addressed some of the lessons I learned along the way, readership blossomed. Other small details make a difference, too. Consistency with regular postings on same days of the week helps draw readers back every week. Add photos to illustrate your topics. Weave in current news topics and be relevant in your discussions or posts.

I have found that one effective way of gaining readers is to do a guest blog for people who are already fairly well established on the blogging scene. When I started, I offered my services to several writers whose work I enjoyed reading. Most were delighted to allow me to appear as a guest on their blog. Their readers read my article, clicked on the links I provided to my blog, and came back if they liked what they saw. That's why I've seen my numbers soar. Blogging is great fun but also a lot of work. Best advice is to stick with it. It takes a good six or eight months before you gain a foothold. I checked the figures on a recent blog and discovered that it received more hits in twelve hours than my entire blog got in the first two months.

You can produce great content, have an attractive blog design, and write regularly—all without attracting a single reader. The real key to starting a blog and keeping it going lies in your ability to connect with your potential audience. You will need a network of social interactions. Think of your blog, not as a monologue or a lecture, but as one side of a conversation. Search for bloggers who are talking about the things you are interested in. Follow the ones you enjoy reading. Comment on their content as frequently as possible. And when someone tries to open a conversation with you, respond to comments and emails quickly. Readers will come back to your blog again and again if they feel they know you as a person.

$\infty\hspace{-0.2em}\backsim\hspace{-0.2em}\infty$

Blogging for Money

I've also been asked how to go about making money from a blog. My first response is to skip lightly over any question about monetizing a blog, because I've never attempted that. I know that a few people blog directly to make money and are successful at it. Those folks, however, already have a huge blogging audience before they start carrying ads and making money. Producing your worthwhile material comes first. Getting readers comes next. Once thousands of people read you every day, you might be able to get rich. Until then, however, I would put that goal aside and concentrate on building a good blog.

If, however, you are determined to try to turn your blog into a cash cow, there are several things you need to understand. First, almost all bloggers who expect to make money from a blog will fail. They fail because they are amateurs at marketing and half-hearted in their efforts to monetize their sites. You can't put up one little ad in a corner somewhere and hope readers will click on it often enough to generate a cash flow. You will have to choose the products you advertise with care, so that they appeal to your specific readers. Don't try to sell sporting goods on a writing blog; try pens or computer software instead. Be sure that what you advertise is reputable and of high quality. If your reader goes to your site and buys a pen that doesn't write, you will receive the brunt of the anger by losing a reader.

You can't run your blog as a business if you are computer-illiterate. You will have to be able to use blog publishing software and social networking sites. You must understand such things as HTML coding, RSS syndication, SEO (search engine optimization) tagging, pings, and trackbacks. And if those terms mean nothing to you at this point, you're not ready to monetize your blog.

Even the host of your blog is important. If you choose a sponsored blog, you need to know how much control the host will give you over your postings. Don't try to sell items on a blog if you do not own the URL of that blog. WordPress is a good choice; I would avoid Blogger because of the URL issues. I use a paid hosting service that lets me sell items through PayPal, but

I cannot use ads provided by Google's Adsense. The arrangement suits me, but it may not suit you.

All of those warnings bring us back to the original point. For most people blogging is not a way to make money. It is, however, a great way to get your name out there. Many publishing companies now insist that their authors have blogs because a great blog provides a potential reading audience for the next book you write. In the long term, your blog may increase your income, but it will probably be a catalyst, not a direct revenue source.

᠗᠑ᢕ᠗

Making Social Media Work for You

There are dozens of social media sites on the Internet, and I am certainly no expert on all of them. The big three—the ones most often used—are Facebook, Twitter, and LinkedIn. They serve different purposes, and I've been surprised to see how different their audiences are. I'll try to show you how I use each one to promote my work, and you can apply the same lessons to another site if you like.

Let's start with Facebook, which now advertises that it has 500 million users. You probably even know a few of those users yourself. I have no intention of telling you how to use Facebook. As I write, the powers behind the scenes are still reorganizing and tweaking what materials you can see, and what others can see about you. If you're going to use Facebook, that's the first thing you'll have to get used to. It changes. Sometimes it changes several times a day.

On my own Facebook account I have discovered close to 400 "friends." They include a few family members; a neighbor or two (although that strikes me as silly); some long-lost high school classmates; several former students, some dating back over twenty years; and a fairly large contingent of academics, mostly medievalists. The rest are members of Lions Clubs or members of the Military Writers Society of America, both locally and around the world. What can they possibly have in common? I know

33

them. I'd recognize them on the street. I'd probably hug most of them. They are all people with whom I have shared both common interests and common experiences. We've worked together, struggled with the same problems, and shared our ideals and goals. I care about them and how they are doing, and I hope they care about me.

When it comes to posting my status on Facebook, I try not to bore my friends or irritate them unduly with efforts to sell my latest book. But if I have had a wonderful day—or a miserable one—these are the people with whom I can share it. I post pictures here, both of myself, so they can watch me age, and of my current activities. It is on Facebook that I am most open about my personal activities and opinions. What good does that do for business, you may wonder? Many of my friends will buy my books; even more will be tickled for me when I win an award. I receive a benefit when they talk about me or leave a congratulatory note on my wall. Facebook friends can form a virtual cheering section in our lives, and that's important.

There's another side to Facebook, too, one that is still evolving too rapidly to lay down strict guidelines here. Anyone with a personal Facebook account ought also to be aware that it is possible to build extra Facebook pages that advertise your business, or your favorite non-profit, or your club. On those pages, you can reach beyond your personal circle of friends to tap into those mysterious 500 million users who are reportedly out there. If you're new at the game, develop your personal page first, and then think about expanding to these "fan pages."

My second social media outlet is LinkedIn. As I indicated earlier, this site is much more business-like than Facebook. I have almost 300 connections on LinkedIn, and almost none of them are cross-overs to my list of Facebook friends. I know less than half of them personally. My LinkedIn connections are the power-brokers in my world. There are a few former students, but they are not the ones who want to reminisce about college life. These are graduate students, or lawyers, or business people who are making a difference in their world. They've sought connections to bolster their resumes. Many of my connections are members of Lions Clubs International, but, again, they are the leaders in that organization—former international officers, staff members, or CEOs of Lions-associated non-profit organizations. They are people I can turn to when I need business-type advice. The rest are business figures with whom I have had some contact, and media and public relations people.

How can they help build my publishing platform? Well, my financial advisor, my lawyer, and my accountant are on that list, along with public figures who can orchestrate newspaper or TV coverage when I have an announcement of a new book or an award. They are the people who can help set up book signings or public speaking engagements. They are great contacts because they have their own contacts. I try not to bury them beneath my sales pitches, and I don't overtly try to sell them anything, but I can trust them to help me make my name better known. Name recognition is a vitally important resource offered by LinkedIn. Another great advantage of LinkedIn is that it lets people with common interests form discussion lists, where they can connect with people who have similar interests or who are facing similar problems. I currently participate in several writers' groups, as well as one that discusses fund-raising ideas for non-profits.

And then there is Twitter. What can you possibly accomplish with 140 spaces? The easy answer, of course, it that it teaches you to cram a lot of information into the smallest possible space. Brevity is good. But beyond that, I see Twitter as a conduit— the vital link between me and the huge world of the Internet. At the moment I have around 800 followers on Twitter, and I'll be the first to admit that I don't know many of them. We are strangers who have made a brief connection because of a third party who knows us both, or because we have a common involvement. They are simply people who have indicated an interest in what I might have to say. When they follow me, anything I post will automatically appear on each of their Twitter feeds. They may, or may not, ever see it. But when they do, they each have the option of passing it on to their own followers, giving my message access to untold numbers of readers. Twitter also has the ability to post automatic messages for me, and to re-post my messages to my other social media outlets.

Here's how it works. Suppose I've finished a blog post announcing the publication of a new book and including a link to the book's order page. I send it to my 800 followers, and Twitter also posts it on my Facebook page (+400 readers) and my LinkedIn profile (+300 readers.) Then a dear fellow writer in England retweets it to her whole list (+1000 readers), the president of a writers' society to which I belong retweets it to her list (+1250), and three faithful blog followers in Missouri, California, and Colorado send it to all their followers (+1700 total). That one personal message reaches over 5000 people within minutes. That's the best, and easiest, advertising I know.

4. Sample New Software Choices

One of the virtues of modern computers is their ability to handle chores that used to eat up days, perhaps weeks, of our working lives. Programmers are constantly working to devise new programs to meet our every need. But, of course, one of the drawbacks of modern computers is that their abilities and services expand too quickly for most of us to absorb. I started this chapter with reluctance, because I'm well aware that anything I recommend today may well be outdated and old-fashioned by the time you read this book. Still, I can't tell you to go out and get whatever is the newest program on the shelf. You want to know not only what's new, but what works.

So here are my current recommendations. Take them for what they are, and nothing more. Concentrate on the features that are most useful, and let those features guide your own purchases.

❧

An Ode to Scrivener

I use Scrivener as my software for novel writing. Those of you who have participated in National Novel Writing Month may already be familiar with it, because the company helps sponsor that annual orgy of writing bliss. Now that Scrivener is available for both MAC and Windows, I can't imagine anyone needing anything else. It's an endlessly versatile program that manages to keep almost every item of the book-writing process in one spot.

There's a section for research, which can hold notes, pictures, maps, and "messages-to-self." I keep lots of pictures there, so that when I am writing about a particular location or character, I can open a picture and keep it on my screen while I write. That adds detail to my descriptions and saves me from making silly mistakes about things like what you can see from a front porch or whether a character sports a mustache.

In fact, it has a whole section for character sketches. You can fill out their questions about each of your characters, defining their back story, their foibles, their nervous quirks, their speech impediments, their hair and eye color, their family relationships— whatever is important to define the character. Then while you are writing, it is easy to click on a character name in the left-hand column and jump to a description.

Scrivener provides a separate template for locations, too, where you can record thing like vegetation, wildlife, smells, sounds. Is your location overgrown with vegetation? You'll need to list what kinds of things grow there. Are bugs important to your story, as they may be for mine? Then you can add their descriptions here. My location files have picture, of course, but also descriptions of the smell of pluff mud and the clicking sound palmetto bugs make as they stomp across a wood floor.

Do you write in chapters or in scenes? Scrivener offers you both options, and once you have all the parts in place, it can put the entire manuscript together for you—in the right order, with chapter numbers. Are you used to working with index cards? Scrivener can display your material in that format, with little cards tacked to a virtual corkboard. You can color code the cards, and you can move them about as you would if you were tacking them to a wall. I used this feature to outline all the chapters of *The Road to Frogmore*. Need more or less writing space? Stretch it out or shrink it. Want a blank screen with nothing but your words filling the screen in front of you? You can do that, too.

Once I've set up the various available folders, my planning stage for the next book is more than complete. I know who's not going to be in the book. I've killed off all the unimportant folks and dumped their first draft chapters and character sketches into a holding tank labeled "Outtakes." They're easily retrievable if I change my mind. Once I'm really sure they are dead, I'll move then to the trash. They're still not gone, however, because the trash doesn't empty until I tell it to. I've identified my main character and some secondary ones who will play important roles. I've outlined all the ideological clashes and the main themes. I have a complete plot outline, with the important points highlighted. Now all I have left to do is write.

∽ා౿ා

Using Dropbox As a Safety-Deposit

Has this ever happened to you? You're in an airport, facing a long delay between flights, and you realize you are going to miss an important deadline. The document you need to submit within hours is on your home computer, and you have nothing with you but your smartphone or a laptop. You need Dropbox.

You've finished deleting a bunch of outdated files, only to discover that you also deleted something important. You're on vacation and want to send some great photos to a friend without revealing your location to all of Facebook. You're in a library with dozens of shelves of books on your research topic, but you can't find your working bibliography. You need Dropbox.

When I was working on my dissertation, back in the day when computers were a rarity rather than a fact of everyday life, one of my professors advised keeping a copy of my dissertation in a fireproof spot. She suggested the oven, since most ovens are well insulated. Her second choice was the freezer. "What will you do if there's a fire in your apartment?" she asked. "Years of work could be turned into ashes in minutes." That was enough to give any graduate student nightmares.

Today, of course, the recurring fear is a computer crash—one unprotected by a backup file. Gremlins attack files without warning. The power goes off before you save. The trash gets accidentally emptied. If you've never lost something you were working on, you are either incredibly lucky or more careful than anyone I know.

I'm sleeping better these days because I now use a simple but elegant program called Dropbox. This form of cloud computing saves and protects anything I store in it. It makes my saved documents instantly available on any computer or mobile device I may be using anywhere in the world. And, if I make changes to one of those documents, it syncs the changes on all my devices. The newest version is always available to me, wherever I may be.

Dropbox offers two gigabytes of storage for free. If you need more than that (and you probably won't), you can purchase 50 GB for $10.00 a month or 20 GB for $20.00 a month. I've been using my basic free version for over a year without coming close to filling it.

꩜

Using Evernote for Everything

The third application in my trinity of necessary software is a program called Evernote. By rights, it should be called Every-Note, because that's what it will hold. Like Dropbox, and to a lesser extend, Scrivener, Evernote uses cloud computing to make sure you are connected to your work, no matter where you are. You can install it on Windows or MAC desktops, almost any smartphone, laptops and notebooks, and tablets such as iPad. Every few minutes, Evernote syncs your files with all your electronic devices. You can start to write an article at your home desk, add notes from your iPhone during a bus trip, stop in the library to add some bibliographic entries, and finish the article at your desk at work. Traveling? No problem. Log onto your account from any computer, and edit that article.

The Evernote design starts with a single note. You give it a title, a tag or two, and start typing. You can attach photos, audio or video clips, data files, websites, and PDFs to that note if you like. Once you have more than one note, you have the beginnings of a notebook, which can hold as many notes as you like. And if you have several related notebooks, you can put them into a stack, which will only count as one of your permitted 250 notebooks.

Let me give you an example of how I use this application. I have a stack for each book I am working on. So, imagine a stack called "The Road to Frogmore." In that stack are several notebooks. One is labeled "Characters." Its individual notes contain character sketches of each character in the book. There are also notebooks for "Plot Points," "Settings," "Historical Events," "Photos," "Maps," and "Bibliography." There are also stacks called "Beyond All Price," "A Scratch with the Rebels," "The Second Mouse Gets the Cheese," and a mysterious one provisionally called "Gus."

But not all my notebooks are related to writing. I have one on "Trips," one for "Recipes," one for "Media Contacts," and one for "Christmas." All the notes are searchable by their tags, even across notebooks. I can turn up a Christmas dinner menu in one and find a recipe for Christmas fruitcake in another. And then I can use those details in a book chapter about Christmas with the Roundheads.

Other Publishing Software Options

Once you've decided to self-publish your next book, your next decision involves choosing a printing or publishing company. We'll go into more detail on that decision later, but at the beginning, I suggest you look at the various free sites available on the web to help you turn your manuscript into a readable format. Here are some options. Take time now to visit their pages and compare their packages and free options. When it comes to releasing your product into the world of readers, there's no such thing as being too well informed.

Amazon KDP. This is the Kindle Store's self-publishing website. It provides full instructions on how to create a Kindle edition and how to upload your book. It also keeps careful records of your sales and royalty payments.

Smashwords. If you publish your book at Smashwords, it will be available at Barnes & Noble, Kobo, Sony eBookstore, Diesel and iBookstore. I have found their services both useful and reliable.

BookBuzzr. This site produces a widget for your book, which you then add to your website, Facebook page, or other social networking sites. You can include part or all of the manuscript—whatever you are willing to offer for free. Clicking on a thumbnail of your book brings up a surprisingly realistic book, complete with turning pages. Once you have signed up, BookBuzzr keeps coming up with new ways to publicize your book. If I had only one publicity choice, this would be it.

Goodreads. The popular online community of readers lets authors also upload e-book files, so they can be read right after they are discovered. It is another good source of word-of-mouth advertising.

❧

Other Writing Resources

Scrivener is definitely my program of choice for writing software. At the same time, I realize that it may not suit your needs. Perhaps you don't have enough hard drive space, or use something other than Windows or OSX. Maybe you don't need all of its features. Here are some other options.

Google Docs. This is a popular office toolbox you can use any time from your Google accounts dashboard. The text editor is pretty basic, but you can share documents online for real time editing and feedback. Download as .txt, .doc, .pdf, .odt and .html. You can access your documents from any device with a web browser by logging in to your Google account.

OpenOffice. This group of productivity tools is available for Windows, MacOS and Linux. Its documents are compatible with all other office suites, including Microsoft Office.

WriteRoom/DarkRoom. If you need a distraction-free editor you have to try WriteRoom (Mac) or DarkRoom (Windows). They get your computer out of the way, so that you can completely focus on your work.

5. Explore Genealogy

If you are into pure fantasy or science fiction, you may skip this chapter. But writers of historical fiction, and anyone who sets a novel in a historical period, may need to consult a genealogist or two. Any time you plan to write about real people, you will need to do some tracking of family relationships. You need to know, for example, if your character is an only child, an orphan, or one part of a huge, closely-knit brood. Sounds like an easy question, doesn't it? Don't be fooled.

~⚬~

What's in a Name?

The first time you visit an online genealogy site, they ask you to enter the first and last name of the person in whom you are interested. Then they suggest you add as many other details as you happen to know. When I was starting the research for *Beyond All Price*, I entered a name (Nellie Chase), her birth state (Maine), and a year range for her birth (1835-1845). And I got results. 147 of them, in fact! Who would have guessed that there would be that many Nellie Chases in the world, let alone in a single state. The site suggested I could narrow my results by entering more information, but more information was what I was looking for. I didn't know her parentage, her city, her death date, her husband's name, or any of the other things they suggested.

Did I eventually find the Nellie I was looking for? Yes, I think so. But it took years, and that will have to be a separate story. Now if you are hunting for a family member, you may have more facts than I did to start out with, but you are likely to run into many of the same problems. Here are some of the pitfalls that you need to be aware of.

Census records look valuable, and they can be, but their worth depends entirely upon the competence of the person doing the recording. I examined a record for my mother's family from the 1900 Pennsylvania Census. It listed the birth dates of two of her sisters as November 1877 and February 1878. Three months apart? Probably not!

For any kind of record before the days of typewriters and computers, handwriting causes major problems. Some examples are marvelously clear; others are scrawls or overwritten with so many corrections that it is impossible to decipher them. Then there are problems caused by mispronunciations or bad hearing or faulty transcriptions. The online version of the 1910 Census shows my mother (Margaret McCaskey) as Marguett Mccacbey.

Nicknames cause their own set of difficulties. Nellie Chase always used the name Nellie, but her given name could have been Nell, Helen, Eleanor, or Ellen. My own brother had problems all his life explaining his name. My mother named him Jack. Just Jack. It was not a nickname, but people naturally assumed that his real name must have been John or Jacques or even James.

Family names change over time. A major culprit may be an immigration record, on which an ethnic name was written down as the closest English approximation. One branch of my father's family bore the surname of Arendt in Germany. They arrived in America as Aurand. Their friends the Muellers became the Millers.

Sometimes name differences are the result of a deliberate choice. I grew up knowing two cousins who sported the same name but different pronunciations. Their fathers had a falling out and did not speak to each other. In an effort to deny their relationship, one pronounced the last syllable of the family name as "KO" while the other used "KAWK." Both, however, spelled it as "-cock."

And then there's my husband's family. We are frequently told that our last name should be spelled "Schreiber." Well, it originally was. The family story says that John Schreiber, who fought in the Civil War, found that his discharge papers had his name spelled wrong. He was given two choices. He could refuse the discharge and stay in the army. Or he could change his name to Schriber, take the discharge as written, and go home that day. He went home! And we've been Schribers ever since.

Don't misunderstand me. Genealogical research is great fun, and you can learn amazing things about your own family, including where all the skeletons are buried. But you do have to enter the search with a healthy dose of skepticism. The best family record sites offer you an option to search for an exact spelling or an approximate one. I usually start with the exact search, but when that fails, a "sounds like" option is frequently the answer. After all, Nellie might have been Nelie, or Nelly, or Ellie, or even Ellen, as she turned out to be.

Here are some online databases that may help your search. Remember, however, that they don't come with guarantees that they are complete or that their information is accurate. I also recommend that you take full advantage of offers to use the sites without charge for a short period of time before committing yourself to paying for a membership. You may find the site useful, of course, but it may contain nothing at all to help you.

- The Social Security Death Index contains birth and death dates for deceased individuals with Social Security numbers who died after 1962 (when the records were computerized) through the current year.
- RootsWeb's WorldConnect Project is a database containing family files submitted by both amateur and professional researchers. For that reason you can expect to find a large number of errors.

- FamilySearch. The Ancestral File and International Genealogical Index (IGI), a service provided by The Church of Jesus Christ of Latter-day Saints, contain information on millions of people worldwide, but these records too can be in error because many contributors are amateurs.
- The Ellis Island Database contains images of ship manifests documenting over 22 million people who entered the United States between 1892 and 1924 through Ellis Island and the Port of New York.
- The USGenWeb Project directory provides links to state and county genealogical resources.
- Perhaps the most useful for the beginning researcher is Ancestry.com. It offers ongoing help, access to millions of handwritten records, and the chance to connect with others who may be researching the same people.

∽೨ల∾

Don't Root Around in Grandma's Attic

Actually, my real advice here is "Don't go rooting around in Grandma's attic until you know enough about what you might find to recognize it when it falls into your lap."

My own encounter with the treasures my Grandmother preserved was a horrible blunder, although I did not realize it at the time. Flash back to a bygone century: I was about nineteen or twenty, home from college for the summer and bored silly. My mother happened to mention that she needed to clean out the attic, and I thought I'd take a look around before she did so.

In a trunk of things she had kept after my grandmother died, I found some amazing old clothes, a beaded evening bag worthy of a Charleston flapper, a couple of Kewpie dolls, and a mysterious white box tied with string. Inside the box, carefully protected from the rest of the objects in the trunk, were items for which I could see no obvious value. (Remember, I was young, stupid, and not yet a history buff.) Three yellow and crumbling newspapers lay on top. All were from Beaver, Pennsylvania—one dated November 23, 1827; one dated December 15, 1841; the other dated January 21, 1846. None seemed to contain anything other than local news, and I didn't spot any familiar names, although each had a handwritten name at the top.

Among the other unexplainable objects were an undated obituary, a red ribbon tied to a blackened medal of some sort, with no discernible legend, a piece of tattered and unraveling gold fringe, a newspaper clipping about a WWI soldier in France, and a single daguerreotype of another soldier. All the other items in the box were letters from people I had never heard of. Each had its own envelope, although the stamps of each had been cut out.

"Odd," I thought, shaking my head at the foibles of old folks who saved such trivial items. I carelessly dropped the whole lot back into the trunk and went downstairs. "Nothing important that I might want," I reported.

Now we fast-forward some twenty years. After my mother's death, I was left to clean out her house. Many of the items I had seen in the attic were gone by then, but I did find the little white box and stuffed it into the parcel of photos I was keeping. The medal, the piece of fringe, and the daguerreotype were not to be found. By then I was a history graduate student, and I began to sift Grandma's treasures with a more educated eye.

I was most excited about a bundle of eight letters, all written during the Civil War. I had been looking for a research project for my American history seminar, and they seemed to hold great promise. And so they did. It took years of reading and researching, but they eventually provided the structure for my book, *A Scratch with the Rebels*, which tells the story of my great uncle, Sgt. James McCaskey, a Union soldier who longed to see military action and died during his first battle.

But what about the rest of the items in Grandma's attic? Well, a few of them helped me with some genealogical research in building Grandma's family tree. I still have not figured out the importance of the newspapers, and their condition continues to deteriorate. There were a few other items that I did not even remember from my first exploration—a poem, the front of a greeting card, a couple of pages from a child's book. But most of all, I regret the loss of the items I did not recognize and preserve.

These are the items that fell into my lap and then slipped through my fingers into oblivion because I did not know what I was looking at. The medal? I think it probably came from WWI and had been awarded to my mother's cousin, the subject of the newspaper clipping. The fringe? Perhaps, although I cannot say for certain, a remnant of one of the battle flags of the 100th Pennsylvania Volunteer Regiment. And the daguerreotype? It was almost certainly the only photograph ever taken of James McCaskey in his Civil War uniform. His family preserved his picture for 120 years; I lost it.

History doesn't come to you neatly packed and labeled with its level of importance. It may be dirty, wrinkled, or crumbling from age. That's what makes it history.

⧲

Do You Have Any Family Skeletons?

A great place to start your search for your own roots is with Ancestry.com. For the beginner, their basic information is free, although you get access to more records if you take out a membership. Recently, NBC ran a series called "Who Do You Think You Are?" in which celebrities got help in tracing their ancestors through the Ancestry records. You could pick up valuable tips by watching on Friday nights at 7:00 PM (EST). Disclaimer: Yes, I am a member of Ancestry.com, although I get nothing for promoting them. In fact, much as I like them, I also want to encourage you to move beyond the materials you find there. They have lots of information, but few family skeletons. For those, you have to look further afield.

Researching your own family tree can be revealing (sometimes too revealing), surprising, or embarrassing. It is almost never dull. The key, I think, is to poke around a lot in all kinds of places and not to start out with a list of specific questions you want to answer. It's much more fun to see what turns up, and then follow the clues until they run out.

Let me give you one small example. Several years ago, when I was starting to write *A Scratch with the Rebels*, I traveled to western Pennsylvania to see what I could learn about my great-uncle James, whose Civil War letters had started me on this adventure. I already had the 1850 and 1860 Census records for Beaver County. (You can actually access some old county lists on line from the U. S. Census Bureau.) I knew the names of his brothers and sisters, their ages, and his father's occupation. I knew James was the second child and oldest boy. The family, however, was still a mystery to me. Even though I looked at the 1860 Census and found my grandfather as the six-year-old Joseph McCaskey, no one in the family seemed real.

Then pieces began falling into place. At the county registrar's office, I learned that the oldest girl, Sarah Jane, had married a man named Simon P. Fisher, and that Simon later served as executor of my great-grandfather's estate when he died in 1875. Then in the local history room of the county library, the curator showed me a map drawn in that same year. It showed every building in the township, each carefully labeled with the owner's name. There— near where I thought it might be—was "Mrs. McCaskey's house." What really caught my eye, however, was the property just down the road. It was a house belonging to Simon Fisher's father, and set way back from the road—hidden from view, almost in the woods—was their barn.

To understand why that was important to me, you have to know a bit about my own teenage years. I grew up in a fair-sized city, back in the days when kids walked everywhere they wanted to go. From the time I was thirteen or so, my mother always sent me out with the same admonition. "You come straight home from school (substitute: movie, dance, play, football game, choir practice, etc.). Don't you think about coming home by way of Fisher's barn." At the time, I thought it was about the dumbest thing she ever said. I didn't know anybody named Fisher, and there wasn't a barn anywhere near our urban neighborhood.

I laughed out loud at discovering the original location of Fisher's barn. My guess? Well, I'm pretty sure that when Sarah Jane and Simon Fisher were courting, they took some detours on their way home. That hidden barn would have made a perfect place for a bit of hanky-panky. And evidently their antics were discovered. I asked around among my cousins, and they too remembered their mothers (my mother's sisters) using the same phrase. In the McCaskey family, Fisher's barn was the equivalent of the local drive-in, the back seat of the family sedan, the back row of the balcony—the local "make out" spot.

It was a bit embarrassing to realize that my mother suspected me of being up to the same sort of shenanigans, but the discovery of the origins of one family saying gave me a warm feeling of belonging. Fisher's barn allowed me to connect with my long-dead ancestors in a way that the usual genealogical charts never could.

ↄ℩ℰↄ

What about Famous Ancestors?

A few weeks later, I asked my Twitter and Facebook friends if they had any family stories about "long-lost cousins" who happened to be famous. Some great stories came out of their answers, all of which confirmed my suspicions that people want to have a connection to the rich and famous, even if it is totally fictional.

My original question arose out of a discovery that Nellie Chase, the main character in the book I was working on, had told her boss that she was a cousin of Salmon P. Chase, an influential member of Lincoln's government. I had checked her family tree, going back six generations, without being able to find a connection. But why would she lie? Well, once I thought about it, I realized that this might be a common human trait. One of my medievalist friends mentioned a student who insisted that she was a direct descendant of Elizabeth I, the Virgin Queen. She saw the contradictions in that but kept clinging to her claim.

That reminded me of the student who bragged to me that he was descended from Charlemagne, an equally implausible relationship, since Charlemagne had only three spinster daughters.

Sometimes the claim does not even refer to the rich and famous. In my father's family, we have a story about a "petrified uncle." It seems he drank himself to death one night, collapsing next to a railroad track. He had so much alcohol in his system that it in effect pickled him. Members of a traveling carnival found his mummified body and carted it off to put into their sideshow as "The Petrified Man." The story says his body traveled with the carnival for years before a member of the family recognized him and dragged him off for a proper burial.

On other occasions, the family legend simply gives a person a much-needed claim to fame. My mother-in-law claimed descent from a signer of the Declaration of Independence without a shred of evidence to back it up, while my father-in-law urged her to claim a relationship to a famous golfer instead because he had more money. My own father, who was always embarrassed that he was a couple of years too young to have served in World War I and too old for WWII, claimed "cousinship" with a famous WWII hero of the same name. I proved that one wrong, but I would never have told him.

So what did I do about my main character? I decided to keep Nellie's claim to fame, because, instead of making her out to be a liar, it makes her all the more human. She apparently let people believe that she had a famous relative, and they had no way of checking out her story (no genealogical databases in the Civil War). Perhaps she even believed it herself. A claim does not have to be true to color how we perceive ourselves and how others perceive us.

6. Know The Difference Between Fact and Fiction

Six years ago, I retired from a career as a college history professor. I had a string of books and articles to my credit and some skills, like deciphering twelfth-century Latin handwriting, that were relatively useless in the real world. What surprised me was discovering that once I was free from the "publish or perish" rule of academia, I still wanted to publish. I knew I had always been a storyteller at heart. The stories behind the history were what fascinated me—not the dates or treaties or economic theories. But was I equipped to write fiction? That, I didn't know. In fact, I'd never thought about the difference between fact and fiction. They were opposites, right? Like salt and pepper, chalk and cheese, good and evil.

Nothing's ever that simple, as I was about to learn.

༺ ❦ ༻

The Role of Research

As a writer, I have a streak of perversity. No, I'm not into kinky sex scenes or ghoulish fantasy. My own brand of perversity is yielding to the temptation to write something I'm not supposed to be working on.

When I was in grad school, starting to work on my dissertation, I was fascinated by the character of the Norman bishop whose career I was supposed to be studying. I had 134 of his personal letters to provide satisfaction for my curiosity. To me, the bishop was one of those people you love to hate. I knew I couldn't believe a thing he said. He didn't call what he did "lying," I suppose. He just told each person exactly what he wanted to hear. He was perfectly capable of telling the king that his son was plotting against him. Then he could turn around and offer the prince his help in overthrowing his father. He was a hypochondriac, inherently lazy, overly interested in his own personal wealth, and a complete coward when danger threatened. What a great villain he would have made! I could have had a wonderful romp telling his story.

Opposing my views was my dissertation advisor, standing over my shoulder and cautioning, "Read the charters, Carolyn. Don't listen to what the bishop says. Read what he does." My supervising committee wanted theory, historiography, background, economic developments, analysis of the architectural changes he introduced—everything except his personality. I finally caved in to their demands, of course, or I wouldn't have gotten my degree. But inside was that little voice that said, "Just you wait! One day I'll tell the real stories."

I continued the scholarly (read "stodgy") writing for fifteen years, always wanting to be more of a storyteller than the academic world would allow. The classroom was my only outlet, and I admit to telling some favorite scandalous stories to some of my upper-division classes. But retirement held out the real promise to me. At last I could let my imagination run free. I could write what I wanted to write.

So here I am, six years into my retirement and embarked on a new career as a novelist. My next book will be about a small group of abolitionists who travelled to South Carolina in 1862. Their purpose? To work with the slaves whose masters had abandoned them when the Union Army captured Port Royal Sound and Hilton Head Island. They are a motley bunch—a novelist's dream. There are both men and women, young and old, religious zealots and fiercely independent Unitarians. They think they have a common goal, but each individual has a different plan for reaching that goal. Their petty squabbles, personal animosities, and dirty tricks furnish enough material for a really juicy novel.

Enter Perversity, stage left. What am I doing with my writing time? I'm deep into scholarly research. I'm still studying people, and the sources of my information are, for the most part, their own letters, diaries, and journals. But now it's my own inner voice that keeps warning, "Read the newspapers, the military dispatches, and the Congressional Record, Carolyn. Don't listen to what the gentleman says. Read what he does."

Could I tell their story with no more information than whatever their letter collections provide? Certainly. But would I be satisfied with the result? Probably not. The curse (or blessing) of an author with historical training is the need to get the facts straight first. Then the story can almost tell itself. More important, that nagging voice is actually making a promise to a future reading audience: "You can trust what you read here. I've done my research."

❦

The Facts Behind the Fiction

Making the switch from academic historian to historical fiction author required some fundamental changes in how I looked at writing. I had to re-think what was most important about the story I was trying to tell. I no longer had to document my research or prove a point. Believe me, giving up footnotes after a lifetime of teaching careful documentation was painful. But then I remembered a prescription one of my own advisors gave me in graduate school. "If your footnote contains information about your story, put it in the story," he said. "If it's simply a reference to your source, and if it's an indisputable fact, leave it out. Only footnote those ideas or details that are likely to antagonize some important old goat looking for a reason to be cantankerous." Voila! My footnotes disappeared. And good riddance.

Other parts of my academic training, however, were impossible to jettison, and I think my writing is stronger because of it. First, I accept the fact that there are restraints on my imagination. I will never write a book about werewolves or space aliens, for example. I might enjoy reading such a tale, but my own flights of fancy never stray beyond the possible. I can create a character and then imagine how she will react in a given situation. I might even be able to write a story from a cat's point of view. But all my characters will resemble, in some form or other, people (or cats) I have known or observed in real situations. I'm stuck with a focus on facts. Don't ask me to write a scene in which a six-eyed robot ends up in a fourth dimension. Even composing the preceding sentence strained my imagination. Fantasy? Can't do it.

Next, I believe strongly in doing one's homework, and I hold writers to a strict standard of accountability. A historical novel must be historically accurate. Nothing irritates me more quickly than finding that an author has changed the facts to suit herself. There's a famous award-winning movie, in which a newly-crowned king of England marries a French princess who immediately gives birth to the heir to the throne. He's a real king, she's a real French princess, and the child does indeed inherit the throne. But the movie sets the marriage some fifteen years too early, when said princess was three years old. If it starts out with a horrible error, why should someone watch the rest of the film? Sorry!

Now that I'm writing about America's Civil War, my desk always contains three types of resources. There's a multi-year calendar of the war, which allows me to check every date and keep the chronology straight. A small pile of books offer details of clothing, furniture, tools, and recipes from the 1860s, so that one of my characters does not sample a dish or use an invention before its creation. I don't hesitate to "Google" details to make sure my characters are believable. To keep the dialogue true, I have a dictionary of nineteenth-century vocabulary that I cannot do without. I even have a handbook of the native flora and fauna of South Carolina, so that I can describe my scenery accurately.

To my delight, I've found that such facts do not usually bore readers. Small details may pass a reader's attention unnoticed, but the cumulative effect of factual knowledge is an increase in plausibility. My historical focus functions as a familiar hook on which a great story can hang.

∽∘∾

Some Rules for Historical Fiction

Here are some of my rules for writing historical fiction. They may not apply to all writers, but they guide me in the choices I make and the kinds of research I do. Read them first. In a later chapter, I'll show you how these helped me choose which of several primary sources would become my writing guide for my newest book.

Be true to the time period. Don't ever guess at the order in which events took place. Double-check dates and times so that you don't run a chance of turning a cause into an effect. There's a difference between saying that a man shot a dog because the dog attacked him, or that the dog attacked the man who tried to shoot him. In the first instance, we're dealing with a vicious dog; in the second, the man may be the one who is vicious.

If your story is about people who live in a particular time period, be sure you know the appropriate details of dress, food availability, household furnishings, modes of transportation, and social customs of the period. Also check details of local vegetation, climate, and wildlife habitats. Don't let your native of Oklahoma pull a salmon out of the local river.

If your story also involves actual political or military events, your responsibilities multiply. Your descriptions and discussions must reflect the facts as they were known at the time. Don't let hindsight lead you astray here. We now know that a pregnant woman who takes the drug thalidomide runs a grave risk of birth defects in her unborn child, but the doctors who prescribed the drug to cure morning sickness back in the 50s did not. Don't blame someone for lack of knowledge if that knowledge was unavailable at the time.

Be true to your story. Most historians hate playing "what if" with history. No matter how many alternative universes you may describe, it won't change the one in which your events actually took place. What if Germany had won World War II? Maybe Hitler would have managed to turn the entire world population into blond, blue-eyed Aryans. Maybe he would have turned out to be a really nice guy whose genetic experiments resulted in the cure of cancer and other life-threatening diseases. Or maybe he would have been hit by a bus, and we would have discovered that we didn't need to fight that war after all. Now we're talking fantasy, not history. And while fantasy may be amusing, it doesn't increase anyone's understanding of anything.

Don't change the facts to suit your story. Change your story to make it fit the facts. The people who read your historical fiction may be people who know the period well. Or, if they don't know much about the history, they are probably hoping to learn something from your story. It's foolish to try to hoodwink readers of the first type, because they will dismiss you as clueless. It's unkind to mislead readers of the second type, because you will be betraying their trust. Either way, you will lose readers, not gain them.

Most important, be true to your character. If you are writing about a real person, you owe it to yourself and to her to find out as much as possible about her. Don't exaggerate her education or experiences. Work with her own life to make her struggles more understandable. Don't rely solely on gossip or what others thought about the character. Ask what she thought about herself. That's why diaries and personal letters are helpful when you are trying to flesh out a character.

Judge the characters in your story only as you could have judged them in person. You must not criticize someone who made a well-considered decision simply because it turned out badly. You need to look beneath the result to discover the intention. Don't blame Lincoln for not emancipating the slaves earlier. You must try to understand what he hoped the Civil War would accomplish before you can judge his efforts. Before you judge a slave-owner, you must at least try to understand why he needed to have slaves in the first place. Only then can you start to examine his treatment of those slaves.

Finally, let your characters be real. Nobody's good and kind all the time. We all have thoughts and temptations we're not proud of. We all have weaknesses. At the other end of the scale, nobody's pure evil. The meanest boss may have a penchant for big-eyed puppies. A kid who terrorizes the neighborhood has a mother who loves him. A cold and distant mother will willingly sacrifice her life for her child. Don't try to gloss over the unattractive elements of your character's personality. If she's perfect, everyone will hate her by the end of the first paragraph. Your readers want real people—people with whom they can identify, people they understand because they recognize them.

∽ℴ℘∾

You're Never Too Old to Learn

Did you know that several battles of the Civil War have two names? Was it Manassas or Bull Run? Elkhorn Tavern or Pea Ridge? Boonsboro or South Mountain? Shiloh or Pittsburgh Landing? Murfreesboro or Stones Mountain?

No, the names are not designed to drive history students crazy. Historian Shelby Foote once speculated that the South named battles for the closest town because most of their soldiers came from rural areas and noticed signs of civilization. The North, however, named battles for nearby bodies of water or other natural landmarks because they came from an urban environment and were attracted to nature.

Now, I had known about these naming difficulties for a long time, and I had protested to a college professor about the unfairness of battles having two names. "It's bad enough to have to memorize the names of the battles," I complained, "without there being two right answers." Knowing why the names were different didn't make them easier to learn, but at least I quit seeing them as a diabolical plot aimed at making me flunk history.

Recently, I taught myself another lesson—this one about applying what you know to the real world. I "knew" battles could have two names. Why, then, did it never occur to me that the one battle I had researched really well might also be known as something else?

I suppose that needs a bit of background explanation. Those of you who have read my books know that *A Scratch with the Rebels* focuses on The Battle of Secessionville. *Beyond All Price* also uses Secessionville as a major turning point in the story of Nellie Chase. I've read almost anything that has been written about that battle, although that's not saying a great deal. It's an episode that history books frequently skip, both because it was such a hugely bungled effort and because it had relatively little impact on the course of the war in general. Yes, it destroyed lives, and changed lives, and altered the nature of the 100th Pennsylvania Volunteers, "The Roundheads." It also delayed the Union plans to attack Charleston by denying them clear passage across James Island. In the long run, however, nothing was accomplished on either side. Even *The New York Times* dismissed it, saying it would probably be best to forget about the disgraceful affair.

So I never realized that the name "Secessionville" stuck to the skirmish of June 16, 1862 on James Island, South Carolina, only because that's what the Confederate Army called it. The name was taken from a nearby summer resort town known as Secessionville. As far as I was concerned, the Union soldiers called it that, too, and in my books, I have them all referring to the event as Secessionville. Until I discovered I was wrong.

I was leisurely reading a passage from Laura Towne's handwritten diary, in preparation for writing the next chapter of *The Road to Frogmore*. The date of the entry was June 22, 1862; the location was the army camp at Hilton Head Island, and specifically, the residence of Gen. David Hunter, whom I have held at least partially to blame for the Union loss "at Secessionville."

Laura Towne had come to Hilton Head from St. Helena Island, accompanying some Philadelphia visitors who were headed home after visiting the Gideonites. She writes:

Gen. Hunter asked us to dine and drove us out to the camp of the black regiment which he reviewed in our honor. After our return, we saw Mr. McK{im} and Lucy off, the steamer being crowded with sick soldiers and the wounded from the Battle of Stono.

Now, the presence of wounded soldiers did not surprise me. I knew that forty-seven soldiers were wounded so badly at Secessionville that they were evacuated and transported to New York City aboard the steamer *Ericsson* several days after the battle. But "The Battle of Stono"? That was news.

Yes, what I've been calling the Battle of Secessionville was also known at the time as the Battle of Stono. Laura Towne could only have heard that name from General Hunter himself. Why would he have called it Stono? Well, true to the rule, the Yankee general must have named it after the Stono River, where Union gunboats managed to break through the Confederate defenses and sail up the river to provide backup fire power for the Union assault on James Island. I'm guessing the name "Stono" didn't stick because northerners were not anxious to talk about a battle in which they were thoroughly trounced.

I never thought much about the issue of which name (north or south versions) becomes the accepted label for a battle. In the light of this discovery, however, it seems that winners got naming rights, while losers looked elsewhere for conversation.

Not Everyone Wants Facts

I was excited and proud to have found out that at least a few contemporaries of the Battle of Secessionville (June 16, 1862) had referred to it as the Battle of Stono. That was the historian in me, showing up to demand that my novelist persona pay attention to the facts. Now, I admit that those two facets of my writing career are often in conflict. When I'm writing history, I want to know (or make up) the story beneath the cold hard facts. I can't indulge that temptation, of course, except when I put on my novelist hat. And then, right in the middle of imagining a great scene, I find myself shuffling off to verify the facts. A historical novelist must be both, and it is not an easy chore.

In this instance I was so excited that I pasted a copy of my article onto a Facebook page, one followed by a small group of descendants and enthusiasts from one of the Union regiments involved in the Battle of Secessionville. I thought they would be "interested" and they were. But at least one of them became defensive and somewhat argumentative about it. As a result, I received both public and private messages during the ensuing discussion.

My biggest critic used a pseudonym in his comments, but I was aware of who he really was and that he had written a book about our mutual topic. His book was straight history; mine was a historical novel. Therefore, he pulled his historical persona on me—reminding me that the "official" records showed no instance of anyone ever using the term "Battle of Stono." I felt like a small child being called to the principal's office to have my fingers slapped. The quirk in our argument is this: he is not a historian by training or occupation, while I am. The question raised became one of methodology. What constitutes "evidence' for a historian? And do incontrovertible facts ever exist? I would argue that everything can be material for a historian, and that any fact labeled " the official version " is likely to be full of distortions, if not downright lies.

I was ready to let the discussion die, but I can't let it go without one more revelation. A day or two later I found another term for this relatively unknown battle. I was reading one of the various editions of the Laura Towne diary, and my discovery of the Battle of Stono came from the Xeroxed copy of her handwritten diary—the one I eventually decided was most authentic. The reference staring up at me on my desk on this day was the printed 1912 (expurgated and propagandized) edition. It read: ". . . the steamer being crowded with the wounded and sick from the battle of Edisto."

Where in the world did that come from? There are three battles associated with the island of Edisto, SC—The Battle of the Tory Camp in 1781, the Battle of Rivers Bridge in February 1865, and the Battle of the Little Edisto on March 28, 1862. All three of them have been called the Battle of Edisto. But this description of the wounded and sick was written on June 23, 1862. The wounded cannot have been lying around in the swamps of South Carolina for three months waiting to be taken to a northern hospital. And there is independent evidence of forty-seven wounded soldiers from Secessionville being loaded onto a steamer to be taken to New York for treatment within days of the June 16th battle.

No, I don't believe for a moment that the Battle of Secessionville was ever called the Battle of Edisto. Both date and location are all wrong. Where did this idea come from? Well, the editor of the Towne letters was not a historian, either. He was a lawyer by training and a writer of children's edifying literature by occupation. I suspect he, too, looked at the handwritten manuscript, saw the term Battle of Stono, and shook his head. Because he had never heard of it, he looked for another possibility. Since the Battle of Secessionville is not exactly a household word, he simply found another battle that took place in that part of South Carolina and "corrected" the silly woman's error.

That's how "historical facts" come out wrong, folks.

7. Do Your Homework

The trouble with telling a writer to "Do your homework" is that there is no one to assign that homework. For many researchers, the search for facts stops at the library door or the local bookstore. But knowledge is not easily corralled. It lies hidden in Grandma's attic, or the local antique shop, or the family cemetery, or a crumbling newspaper clipping. An aspiring historian, or a historical novelist, must be ready to snatch a fact out of the middle of a pile of nonsense. She must be open to discoveries found in the strangest of places. Here are a few examples.

❧

Carved on a Rock

On May 5, 1868, General Logan, commander of the Grand Army of the Republic, issued an order declaring that Union and Confederate war dead would be honored on May 30 with flowers laid on their graves in Arlington National Cemetery. That was the origin of Decoration Day, or, as we are more apt to call it, Memorial Day. In cemeteries all over the country, small G.A.R. markers stand next to larger stones, and in May veterans and scouting troops plant a small American flag near each marker. There's no better time to go looking for a Civil War burial site.

My mother's family had its own Civil War soldier to honor, and, when I was young, Decoration Day was the traditional day for the family to gather in North Sewickley Cemetery, right outside Ellwood City, Pennsylvania, for a day of cleanup and family reminiscing. Five McCaskey sisters, accompanied by picnic baskets, flower pots, rakes, hoes, grumbling husbands, and assorted children spent the day moving from gravestone to gravestone, not mourning but celebrating the good times they remembered.

I learned my family's history during those yearly excursions to North Sewickley. There was the marker of the family matriarch, who brought her seven children from Ireland to the hills of Pennsylvania in 1795, traveling first in steerage, and then on foot. Her stone bore only the single word, "Nancy," but it still stands firmly rooted on that hillside. A small stone marks the grave of cousin Electa, believed to have died in the flu epidemic of 1918 (although the stone says 1917); another grave memorializes a tiny James McCaskey, a victim of diphtheria at the age of two in 1896. By noon, the decorating crew had usually made its way to a circle of pine trees near the graves of the McCaskey sisters' grandparents. Lunch was spread on blankets while someone told the story of Sgt. James McCaskey, who died in defense of his country in 1862. Long before I found the official account of James's death, I knew the story of the brave young man left sitting up against a tree on the battlefield while he bled to death from cannon fire.

Cemeteries can prove to be a rich source for genealogical research. But as always, a researcher must accept any such evidence with a high degree of skepticism until it can be confirmed. Here are some suggestions for doing your own cemetery explorations.

Gather as much information as you can before you actually visit the cemetery, unless, of course, you're curious and not looking for anything or anyone in particular. Assuming you are interested in specific individuals, start by asking questions. If you know the cemetery you plan to visit, check with the caretaker or sexton to see if there is a directory. If the cemetery is no longer an active one, look for the pastor of the nearest church. Or try the local history section of the public library.

An obituary from a local newspaper can tell you which cemetery to visit. That's how David Welch and I eventually found the grave of Nellie M. Chase. Her obituary, reprinted in a Reading, PA newspaper, said she was living in Paris, TN at the time of her death. It also suggested that she and her husband ran the railroad hotel there. The obituary noted that both of them actually died in Louisville, KY. That information led to a local newspaper article about yellow fever deaths in Paris, TN. Other yellow fever articles led to a book on their employer, the L & R Railroad, which in turn gave the name of the cemetery in which Nellie and her husband were buried. After that it only took a quick inquiry to the Cave Hill Cemetery in Louisville to discover the exact location of their burial plots and to get a photograph of their joined headstones.

Take the right equipment with you. Plan to take notes on every headstone you identify, but also be sure to have a camera. Notes have a way of perpetuating small errors. You'll want a picture later to double-check the details. Traditionally, Christian graves are oriented toward the east; i.e., the headstone is at the west end of the plot and the foot of the coffin at the east end, in preparation for Resurrection Day. For that reason, inscriptions on a headstone will be clearer if the picture is taken in the morning.

Don't forget the insect spray. Mosquitoes can be formidable guards against your investigations. And unless the cemetery is well maintained, take gardening gloves and pruning shears. I really wanted to try to straighten Uncle James's headstone, but a crop of fresh poison ivy dissuaded me. A spray bottle of water also comes in handy. Inscriptions are easier to read when they are wet, and you may need to wash away soil accumulations.

Be alert to the clues on the stones themselves. Carvings on the headstone may provide clues to religion or military service. Children's markers are likely to have flowers or small animals. I like to think the little figure on Cousin Electa's stone is a rabbit.

Tombstones frequently bear birth and death dates, although birth years are less to be trusted than death years. An inscription reading "Beloved Wife" usually means the woman's husband was still alive at her death. Stones reading "Mother" and "Father" confirm the existence of children alive at the time of the parents' deaths.

Unmarried sons and daughters are more likely to be buried near their parents. The graves of a woman or a couple near small, unmarked stones may indicate the deaths of unnamed infants. Death dates can tie a victim to a natural disaster such as an earthquake or an epidemic of influenza or yellow fever.

Note the names on graves close to those of your own family members. You may be looking at their friends and neighbors. Cemeteries have many stories to tell. Let the stones speak to you.

⁓৹৻⁓

Where Did They Put Grandpa?

I have learned a lot about cemetery research from a mysterious headstone that bears the name of my great-uncle James McCaskey, who was killed in the Civil War. After much searching, I found this marker in the same Pennsylvania cemetery where many of my other McCaskey ancestors are buried. It reads:

James McCaskey
Born April 12, 1839
Died June 16, 1862
James Island, S.C.

Those details are all correct; the military action on James Island was the Battle of Secessionville. The problem is that the notification of his death says that his body was never found. The official records say that the Confederate troops buried the Union soldiers killed in the battle (some 509 of them) in unmarked graves on the battlefield. North Sewickley Cemetery records indicated that the headstone was placed in 1875, after Mrs. Jane McCaskey purchased three adjoining plots and ordered three matching stones—one for her recently deceased husband John, one for herself, and one for her missing eldest son James.

Sure enough, the marker next to the one for James marks the grave of my great-grandmother Jane McCaskey. But on the far side of her grave, the ground has been cut away, and a gravel road lies several feet below the resulting ledge. Where is Great-Grandpa John? There is no sign of him or his tombstone at all. Was he ever there? Did an earthmover carry him away when the road was put in? Or is he in the plot marked with his son's tombstone? At this point the solution to the problem becomes too macabre to consider. I am willing to accept what I think I know without further investigation.

Lesson Number One: A tombstone does not always equal a real burial. Obviously, James's headstone marks an empty grave, a not uncommon phenomenon during a war that swallowed up thousands of young men on distant battlefields. The Grand Army of the Republic honors James McCaskey's service every Memorial Day by placing a flag on the grave site, but even their records stop short of stating that he is actually buried there.

Lesson Number Two: The lack of a headstone does not necessarily mean that no grave ever existed. As time passes, stones crumble, weeds take over, land subsides, new demands for gravesites force owners to change the layout of their cemetery plots. Jane McCaskey's stone now teeters dangerously close to the edge of the cut-away bank. In fact, it is largely supported by the roots of the tree growing behind the stone. John's grave would have been on the far side, since wives were nearly always buried to the left of their husbands. John has disappeared, but we know from court records and other documents that he was buried in that location in 1875.

Lesson Number Three: Burial practices change over time. While I was planning this blog post, I received a message from another genealogist, a distant cousin of my husband, who had found the graves of my husband's grandfather and great-grandfather. I was astonished to learn that both men were buried in the same grave at St. Mary Cemetery in Cleveland, Ohio—one above the other. The cemetery records show John Christoph Schreiber (1845-1889) in section A, lot 48 North grave 4 E.D. (which stands for extra deep, or at about eight feet). His son, John C. Schriber, Jr. (1867-1928) is in section A, lot 48 North, grave 4 O.T. (on top, or at about 4 feet).

Cemeteries can tell us a great deal about those whose lives we are researching. Sometimes, perhaps, they tell us more than we really wanted to know!

∽∘⌒

Don't Believe Everything You Read

Recently the Internet has given researchers access to literally millions of pages of old newspaper articles. Unfortunately, newspaper articles are as likely to be misleading as any other source. Consider this example, which turned up while my favorite researcher was looking for information about the 100th Pennsylvania (Roundheads) Regiment:

Altoona Times (Altoona, PA) March 4, 1864

"In the early part of the present month, a soldier belonging to the 100th regiment, having reenlisted for the war, obtained a thirty days' furlough and returned to his home in Lawrence county, about four miles from Darlington, and almost adjoining the Beaver county line. The man was married, and during his absence his wife contracted an acquaintance with a scamp in the neighborhood, which culminated in a criminal intimacy between the parties. Of all this, however, the husband was in complete ignorance, and upon his return home he took up his abode with his wife, unconscious of her infidelity or of the plot which was even then maturing against his life.

It appears that soon after his arrival it was agreed between the woman and her paramour that he should be put out of the way, and one night, while the unsuspecting man lay asleep in his bed, the guilty pair approached him, and slipping a noose, which they had previously prepared, over his head, they threw the other end over a beam which extended across the dwelling, and pulling on it with all their might, they swung the wretched man off the bed, and in a moment almost had him in such a position that resistance on his part became impossible. They had their victim now completely in their power; and the deliberation which marked their after movements shows a degree of cold-bloodedness unequalled almost in the annals of crime.

"Finding that death did not take place as soon as they had expected, they fastened the rope, which up to this time they had held over the beam, the body of their victim writhing in his death agony from the other end, to a peg in the wall, and leaving the miserable man to his fate passed out of the house. After remaining outside long enough for strangulation to take place, they again entered the house, and taking down the now lifeless remains of the murdered man carried them to a coal bank in the vicinity, inside which they concealed them.

"The next day it was noticed that the woman's paramour was rather flush of funds, and this, coupled with the fact that the soldier was missing, induced those who knew the guilty relations existing between the woman and the man to suspect that all was not right; an inquiry was instituted through which the entire tragedy was brought to light. The woman, struck with fear or remorse, made a confession of the whole affair, implicating her paramour as the principal in the murder, and both he and she were arrested in committed to jail at New Castle to await their trial for murder.

"The gentleman from whom we obtain our report of the tragedy could not give us the names of the parties, but he vouches for the correctness of the facts as we have given them. It is the most horrible affair, and naturally created great excitement in the community where it occurred."

We were both fascinated. What a great story! Note how many specific details here give further reason to believe the whole tale. We were already combing the regimental rosters to find the soldier who disappeared in early 1864, when the following article turned up:

Evening Telegraph, Harrisburg, PA, March 12, 1864.

"A SENSATION STORY SPOILED. The New Castle Courant spoils the sensation story which has been going the rounds of the press for some days relative to the murder of a soldier at Enon Valley by his wife and paramour. The man did return as stated and discovered the infidelity of his wife, but left the neighborhood, either the same night or early the next morning, and though diligent inquiry was made, was not heard from until Wednesday last, when he turned up, alive and well, at Enon Valley, from whence he went to visit his father in Ohio.

"His sudden disappearance excited fears in the minds of the neighbors, which were strengthened by the fact that his wife and her paramour had his watch and plenty of greenbacks. All the twaddle about the tight rope performance, and the parties or either of them having acknowledged their guilt or been arrested, was hatched in the excited imagination of a Pittsburg paper's informant. The guilty pair have left for parts unknown."

Thus perished a great plot for a novel. Sigh!

∽ℰ∾

Researching the Unknowable

One of the hardest lessons I have had to learn about research is that sometimes you can't find the answers. In a few instances, that may be a good thing, of course, since there are facts that no one wants known. When you need information, however, missing information can be maddening. It's important to know when to stop hunting.

In 1992, I was working on a translated edition of Latin letters written by a twelfth-century Anglo-Norman bishop. One letter in particular was causing me problems as I tried to identify a person referred to only by his name, Milo. Medieval scribes, you see, frequently abbreviated words to save precious vellum, and their abbreviations can be confusing to later readers. In this case, there was a single word with two possible meanings. The word that came before Milo's name had a mark at the end that might— or might not—be the sign of an abbreviation. If that is what it was, then Milo was a messenger or someone who was simply transporting the letter in question. If it was not an intentional abbreviation mark, the sentence identified Milo as the scribe who had actually written the letter. Other scholars had disagreed on which was the correct reading.

Foolishly I decided to solve the mystery. The earliest copy of the letter appeared in a manuscript held by one of the colleges in Oxford. Since I happened to be teaching in a summer program at that college, I assumed it would be an easy matter to get a close-up look at that word and decide for myself whether it was an intentional mark or something accidental, such as a spatter from a rough quill or even a fly speck on the page.

I presented myself at the library soon after arriving in England and found the door barred by the "She-Who-Must-Be-Obeyed" librarian. "No," she said. "You may not come in." Well, she outweighed me by at least a hundred pounds, and when I say she blocked the door, she literally did so. Our little summer program, she told me, was simply renting space at the college. I had no credentials in England; her library was only for "real" scholars or researchers. No amount of pleading by the head of our program would budge her. And that was the end of that.

I was not ready to give up. Milo's identity still puzzled me. Four years later, I went back, this time carrying official letters from my college and from my PhD-granting university. Didn't matter. I still was not getting in. She agreed, finally, to send me a microfilm copy of the manuscript, and a year later it arrived. Problem solved? Nope! You can't identify ink marks from a photo.

Fast forward to 2002. A third trip was in the works, and this time I contacted an English scholar who had been hired by the library to catalog their collection. He graciously interceded for me, and this time, after almost nine years of effort, I received permission to see the original manuscript. My letter ordered me to report to the front door, credentials in hand, on a specific day and at an odd hour and precise minute. "She-Who-Must-Be-Obeyed" met me at the door and stood back to allow me to squeeze past her. She practically frisked me to be sure I wasn't carrying a camera or a pen or pencil. Then she handed me a pair of sturdy white gloves and insisted that I put them on before I entered the reading room. She led me to a desk, where the manuscript lay on a cushion and announced that I had only fifteen minutes to examine it. The entire time, she stood looming over my right shoulder to be sure I did not damage the pages in any way.

There it was, finally—my mystery mark—and I still could not tell for sure. The ink colors were, perhaps, a bit off, which would suggest a later added mark, but I could not tell for sure, and there was no way to magnify it or improve the lighting. If it was a fly speck, as I suspected, I could have discovered that with a simple flick of a fingernail, but the heavy gloves and the looming supervisor made touching it impossible.

So my fifteen minutes passed. I watched the elusive folio disappear from its cushion as I was ushered out the door. No happy ending here. Some things you can't find out, no matter how good your research skills. As a poker player might say, "You have to know when to fold 'em!"

⚬⚬⚬

Layers of Deception

I used to have a bit of fun with my students while trying to make clear the unreliability of so-called facts. "Imagine that it is fifty years in the future and you have become famous for your writing, art, or political commentary. Critics have decided that the crucial moment that set you on the path to success came during the weekend of Mardi Gras in 2001. Don't tell me what you did. Just picture it mentally. What was it? Where is the evidence? Now, what did you tell your best friend about the weekend? And what did you tell your parents? If future biographers look for evidence in your letters, diary, journal, text messages, or Facebook photos, how accurate will their accounts be?" After the blushes and giggles subsided, they got the message.

I'm currently dealing with the same sort of problem. Much of the evidence for the life of Laura M. Towne, the heroine of my next book, must come from her own writings. There are, however, several renderings of those writings. The evidence comes in layers, like an onion, and each time we peel away a layer, the stronger becomes the scent of unreliability.

A published volume offers the easiest way to access Laura's writings. Rupert Sargent Holland edited the whole collection and published it in 1912. It has been reprinted and is available for only a few dollars on Amazon. It reads well and it dates most of

76

the materials, although some confusion results from the editor's failure to distinguish between journal entries and letters—an important distinction, as my students would have recognized. As a result, contradictions crop up—a statement that she has never felt better followed by a complaint of on-going illness, for example. Gaps also exist. Did Laura really not write anything about important events that occurred during those gaps, or did her editor not include what she wrote?

And who is Mr. Holland? As her editor, he necessarily stands between the writer and her words. An Internet friend who has been working on this same material suspects that he may be Laura's nephew. I have spent some time in the genealogical records, and I've been unable to find any connection between Holland and the Towne family. I do know that he was a Harvard-educated lawyer, who also wrote edifying children's books, such as *Historic Boyhoods* and *Historic Girlhoods*. His writings all emphasize those qualities a right-thinking child should emulate. But did he actually censor Laura's writings in any way?

A collection of materials concerning the Penn Center is housed at the University of North Carolina at Chapel Hill. A typescript of Laura's journal and letters is accessible on microfiche in the library. I've not yet seen it, but my Internet friend has. She tells me that the typescript is marred by two problems. The more serious one involves passages in the typescript that have been actually scratched out or marked over for exclusion. Since the marked passages do not appear in the print version, it seems safe to assume that the deletions were made at the time the book was being written. We can't know who made the choices, however. Did a relative tell the editor not to include this bit? Or did the editor decide the excluded passage did not fit with the point he was trying to make? Either way, the reader is hearing a voice other than Laura's.

It would be easiest to blame the editor, but the original typescript has gaps, too, indicated by ellipses (. . . .) showing where material has been deliberately left out. Who created the typescript? We don't know, although there is a reference in the introduction that seems to suggest that Laura may have been the aunt of the transcriber. How did the typist choose what to leave out? Was (s)he influenced by a need to protect her relative?

There's no way to tell without being able to view the originals side by side with the typescript. Laura's letters and journals may still exist, but for the time being they remain out of reach. They have been housed in the Archives at the Penn Center in South Carolina, but they are now in the process of being catalogued and transferred to the University of North Carolina at Chapel Hill. They were pulled from circulation three years ago, and no one seems to know when they will be once again accessible. I've been mourning their temporary loss just when I need them, but I do recognize—as did my students—that what Laura wrote may not have been what Laura felt or did.

Here's one example of how the layers of evidence can change the facts. Laura fell ill during her first year in the Sea Islands, suffering from one of the many swamp fevers. She didn't like to complain to those around her but her medical training led her to record all the nasty symptoms in her journal. And because she didn't want her family back home to worry about her, she told them that she was never healthier. The transcriber keeps both the "I'm healthy" letter and the "I'm dying" journal entry, but omits all the gory details of stomach fluxes and bowel disorders—a typical Victorian attitude toward bodily functions. The book editor spots the discrepancy and makes a choice. He wants his heroine to be a strong woman, so he omits any mention of her illness. And the reader comes away believing that Laura found the Sea Island climate a particularly healthy and invigorating one.

～◦～

Betrayed by Translation

"Always check the identity of your source." The more information becomes instantly available over the Internet, the more careful you have to be. There's a wealth of material out there; there is also a never-ending supply of quacks, polemicists, and other angry people. Don't accept anything without finding some strong supporting evidence.

I want to call attention to a particularly dangerous area—personal letters or diaries that have been transcribed, copied, or edited by someone else. The Italian language has an important proverb: *"Traduttore traditore."* It means, roughly, "a translator is a traitor." Spanish provides a similar thought: *"E que traduce, traiciona,"* or "He who translates is guilty of a betrayal." I kept the Italian version posted on the wall right above my office computer while I was working on a translation of Latin letters, to remind myself that my English translation should reflect nothing but what the author wrote, not what I thought he should have written.

Back when I was first starting to do the research for *A Scratch with the Rebels*, I traveled to Penn State University to sift through a huge collection of materials from the 100th Pennsylvania Regiment. Seven large boxes in the library basement held a conglomeration of original letters, newspaper clippings, and typescript copies of other letters and diaries from members of the regiment. Nothing much had been done to preserve the materials, and the original documents were often faded and ripped. I was grateful for the typescripts and spent much of my limited time reading those because they took less time and effort. The collection as a whole was so valuable for what I was doing that I didn't worry much about authenticity. It had, after all, been collected by other descendants of the Roundheads, and it was compiled by a college English professor who taught in the area from which the regiment had been recruited.

Some time a bit later, I was in the public library in New Castle, PA, this time looking for newspaper articles that would reveal how much the people back home knew of the war and how they felt about it. At one point the librarian came back into the archives to chat. She casually mentioned an elderly gentleman who had been there several years before. He had been looking for evidence that the regimental commander had been having an affair with the regimental nurse. He had insisted that the chaplain had been upset about the affair. Had I seen anything about that, she asked. I dismissed it out of hand. After all, I had just finished reading a typescript of Rev. Browne's letters, and I had not seen a single mention of such a thing. I dismissed it as utter nonsense. The librarian was relieved; Col. Leasure was a New Castle native and a local hero. She wanted nothing to sully his name.

I, too, put it out of my head for the time being, but I became a bit intrigued by the possibility. Col. Leasure was a dapper little fellow. Nurse Nellie was young and attractive. Rev. Browne was a straight-laced Calvinist. When I went to the Military History Institute in Carlyle to investigate their holdings, I was pleased to learn that they had the original letters from Rev. Browne—some three hundred of them, many more than I knew about. I asked for the collection and put my husband to work on one stack while I plowed through the other. "Look for any mention of Nellie," I told him.

It didn't take long! These original letters were full of innuendo, snarling attacks on Nellie's character, and semi-veiled accusations of improper relationships. It was clear that the good chaplain had hated the nurse with a finely-honed passion and that he resented the fact that the colonel seemed to favor her. But why the difference? When I talked to the archivist there, he shrugged and said, "Well, Browne's granddaughter was the one who prepared the typescript before we received the letters."

And there was the answer to at least part of the puzzle. The granddaughter had sanitized the collection, systematically removing anything that might have reflected badly on her beloved ancestor. It didn't prove, of course, whether or not there had been an affair. It simply explained why I had not reached the same conclusion as the elderly gentleman who believed what Browne had believed.

I remain grateful for the discovery. It gave rise to my next book, *Beyond All Price*, and in that novel I had to deal with the question of the affair. I won't give away my final conclusion, but I can tell you that I would have written a much different book if I had not read the original letters for myself.

8. Keep Asking Questions

Recently, Margaret Frazer, one of my favorite writers of historical fiction, posted an article on how to judge historical fiction. She made such a good point that I think it's worth repeating here. If you write a novel about a historical event by taking all the known facts into account, that's historical fiction. If you change an inconvenient historical fact to make a better story, you're writing historical fantasy.

Now there's nothing wrong with fantasy. We all enjoy it occasionally. Along with millions of other viewers, I look forward to a new season of "True Blood." I'm willing to believe that Sookie is a fairy, Bill is a vampire, Sam is a werewolf, and Eric is 4000 years old. It's pure fantasy and good entertainment for an hour or so. But no one will ever confuse it with fact. The principle that governs theatrical performances—the suspension of disbelief—goes all the way back to the ancient Greeks, and who are we to argue with them?

Nevertheless, the writer of historical fiction carries an additional burden. A historical novel must never give its readers reason to believe something that is not true, and it must never destroy a dead person's reputation for the sake of a good plot line. Those requirements are the motivations that send writers like me back to the libraries, archives, and piles of crumbly newspapers. The challenge becomes even more difficult when those resources do not agree on the facts.

❧

The Challenges of Historical Fiction

During the writing of *The Road to Frogmore*, I struggled with a particularly knotty historical problem. I was writing about one of the abolitionist women who went to South Carolina in 1862 to work with newly freed slaves. Laura Towne spent the next forty years of her life in the Low Country. She established the Penn School, which became a model of educational excellence and one that has developed into a major center for the preservation of Gullah culture. I look on her accomplishments with awe.

And yet . . . And yet . . . Trying to write about her became a difficult and frustrating effort. The problem? She kept a diary. Now, under most circumstances, that would be exciting news. A diary provides a way into her innermost thoughts, a way to understand her motives, her doubts, her worries, and her triumphs. In this case, however, there are too many competing copies of that diary, and worst of all, the original little composition books she used have disappeared.

Laura died in 1901. Her best friend and partner in all her efforts, Ellen Murray, died in 1908. Shortly after Ellen's death, Laura's diary became public knowledge. Laura's great-nephew authorized a typescript copy of the diary and circulated it among the trustees of the Penn School. In 1912, a friend of the nephew published an edition of her diary and letters. The book is still available; I purchased my copy on Amazon. Sometime later, it was re-edited and re-issued by the Negro University Press. In the microfilm collection of Penn School Papers, housed at the University of North Carolina Library in Chapel Hill, there are two different typescript copies of that book, one typed on an old manual typewriter, and the other on a slightly more modern electric machine. Both have been extensively marked up, scratched out, and edited. And they do not match either each other or the print editions.

The real purpose of my recent trip to Beaufort was to track down the original diary. Everyone I talked to said, "Oh yes, we have a copy" or "Oh yes, I've seen a copy." A copy. Not the original. But while there, I learned of another copy. This one was purported to be in Laura's own handwriting. It had passed through Ellen's estate to her great-niece, and then to a woman who wrote a history of the school in the early 1980s. She returned the handwritten original to the great-niece after making a Xerox copy. The University of South Carolina now holds the Xerox copy and agreed to make a copy for me.

It arrived—all 212 pages of it—written in a lovely and legible 19th-century hand. Now I could compare it to the print edition to see what changes that editor had made. Problem solved? No way! The two are entirely different in tone and in vocabulary. The attitudes and beliefs stated are sometimes diametrically opposed to one another. In places the handwritten copy is more detailed than the print edition. In others, the print edition contains long passages that are not contained in the handwritten copy. There is no way to determine which one is an abridged version of the other.

Which details are fact and which are fantasy? Somewhere beneath all these various copies lay the real Laura. But could I find her? I wasn't sure.

෴

No Guarantee of Accuracy

I am convinced that the original diary no longer exists or has fallen between the cracks somewhere in a distant family member's attic. Everyone I talked to seemed to "know" where it was—except that they were all wrong. Even the highest-level archivists admit that they cannot produce it. My own explanation? I think it disappeared for the same reason there are four versions of it. Laura's friends and family members had varying memories of her—memories they did not want to challenge by allowing the public to read Laura's most private thoughts. How do you keep her thoughts private? By hiding them away where no one will ever find them. And somebody did a really good job.

If I were still thinking like a historian, I might have been tempted to drop the whole thing right there. A historian must be sure of her sources. If the original is not available, the quest is over. But Dr. Paul Hyams reminded me that saying "There is no evidence" is a historian's excuse, not a defense for a novelist. A novelist must bring imagination to the mix, hoping to come up with the hidden solution. Here's my analysis, somewhat abetted by my own imagination.

Source number one is a microfilmed copy of a typescript of the diary, obviously produced on an electric typewriter and then carefully proofread and corrected with proofreader's marks. I have no idea who typed this version, but I can date it to the 1960s or early 1970s, when electric typewriters were available to writers. That makes this version a hundred years younger than the original. And for that reason alone it is unlikely to be the closest match to the original. In a hundred years, too many other individuals have had a chance to make changes. Out it goes.

Source number two is also a typescript contained on the same roll of microfilm from the University of North Carolina's Southern History Collection. This one differs in several ways. It was typed on an old manual typewriter, evidenced by the slightly misaligned letters, the standard evenly spaced font, and the tendency of some circular letters to be shaded because the typewriter keys have collected ink in their depressions. It is also identified as having been prepared from the original by Dr. Horace Jenks for the information of the Board of Trustees of the Penn School. The approximate date of preparation was 1908, just after the death of Laura's long-time partner, Ellen Murray.

This one called for more investigation. First, who was Horace H. Jenks? He was the son of Helen Carnan Towne, who was the daughter of John Henry Towne, Laura Towne's older brother—which makes him Laura's great-nephew. His mother had inherited Laura's estate in 1901. By the time of Ellen Murray's death, Horace and his older brother Robert were taking over trusteeship duties at the Penn School from their mother. It is safe to assume that both Horace and Robert Jenks had seen Laura's diary; when Horace authorized a typescript, he was working from the original.

But that's not the end of the story, because this typescript has its own problems. It is incomplete. There are gaps in the dating, sometimes for several weeks and sometimes as much as three months. Furthermore, Horace was a Harvard-educated academic, who dutifully used the required ellipses whenever he omitted sections of the diary. The typescript is riddled with those little series of dots . . . . I'm grateful he at least marked them, but omissions simply raise more questions.

Did he leave out the boring parts? No, the omitted sections often occur at times when diaries and letters from other Gideonites reveal great turmoil—internal disagreements, disputes with the army, massive epidemics of killer diseases, or unusual danger from the threats of war. The result is a fairly happy picture of a woman who is doing the job she was sent to do, teaching slaves, treating minor ailments, and learning how to live in a surprisingly hospitable new land. It's a lovely picture, but obviously inaccurate. That's the trouble with ellipses.

One other characteristic of source number two bothered me. In it, Laura frequently expresses her displeasure with—and sometimes outright disgust for— the freedmen of South Carolina. She comments on how dirty they are, how uncivilized, how slow to learn, how uncooperative, how rude, how lacking in ordinary common sense, how superstitious, how cruel in their treatment of animals. Her attitude in the early sections of the diary does not in any way reflect her abolitionist belief that the Negro was as capable as any white person. In later sections, the complaints diminish, but favorable judgments are still hard to find. Why would Horace leave such derogatory comments in the typescript?

Maybe he was being honest. Maybe Laura Towne was a bigot. No, there's a more plausible explanation. As early as 1900, Horace Jenks was leading a movement to change the nature of the Penn School. When Laura founded the school, she wanted it to offer a standard "English" education, so that the children of freedmen would grow up with the same educational advantages as their white neighbors. For almost forty years, she taught academic subjects—sometimes offering Latin, advanced algebra, philosophy, and ancient history. Horace Jenks and several other trustees favored turning the Penn School into a vocational center. They had begun dropping the academics and substituting classes in shoemaking, blacksmithing, basket weaving (really!), sewing, and agriculture. The change reflects the racial biases of the early 20th century, of course, but the edited transcript of Laura Towne's diary gives the erroneous impression that Laura shared those views. Why did it not appear until 1908? I suspect it was because Ellen Murray was no longer around to oppose it.

This typescript has its value, but only for the sake of what it reveals about the editor, not about the original writer. I might use it for comparative fact checking, but it's not a reliable guide to Laura.

⁓⊙⌀⁓

Pretty Is As Pretty Does

Two editions of the Towne diary remain. The printed edition is easy to dismiss. *The Letters and Diary of Laura M. Towne*, edited by Rupert Sargent Holland, was published in 1912. Holland used two sources, a typescript of the diary, which was prepared by Horace Jenks, and a similar typescript of Laura's correspondence, in whose preparation Helen Jenks had a hand. A careful comparison of print edition and the Jenks typescript reveals that Holland, or someone guiding his efforts, made a great many additional cuts in the original material.

Let's start with Holland himself. I have been unable to verify a direct connection between the Jenks family and Holland, except that Horace and Rupert were the same age, both born in 1878, and attended Harvard at the same time, where a friendship between them is at least plausible, if not likely. Holland is best known in the library world as the author of "historic" books such as *Historic Boyhoods, Historic Girlhoods, Historic Ships, Historic Inventions, Historic Railroads, Historic Heroes of Chivalry*. Are you sensing a pattern here? Laura's writings may have barely escaped being titled *Historic Letters and Diaries*. The Holland edition falls into the early 20th-century genre of "edifying literature." Laura is always healthy, always optimistic, always content—never a living mass of contradictions and human failings. I'm sure the resulting volume pleased Laura's family, but as a historical source it is nearly worthless.

By the process of elimination, I was down to a single source—a curious handwritten copy of the diary housed apart from the main collection of Penn Center documents. I found its background reassuring. It is assumed to be a copy of the diary made by Laura herself and given to her long-time companion, Ellen Murray. In 1908, this hand-written copy passed to Ellen's niece, who was the daughter of Ellen's sister, Harriet Murray, and T. Edwin Ruggles, who was also a member of the original Gideonite band of missionaries. Eventually the copy passed to Ellen's great-niece, Helen Shaw.

Helen Shaw loaned the hand-written diary to Edith M. Dabbs, who was helping to catalog and archive the papers at the Penn Center during the 1960s. Who was Edith Dabbs? She was the wife of a Penn Center Trustee who served from 1960 to 1970. After his death, Mrs. Dabbs stayed on as the archivist of the Penn Center. She was an English teacher, the wife of a USC English professor, and a trained journalist. She wrote several books, perhaps the most important of which is *Sea Island Diary: A History of St. Helena Island*, published in 1983. Her primary source material? This hand-written copy.

Mrs. Dabbs allowed the University of North Carolina Library to Xerox the manuscript before she returned it to Mrs. Shaw. Mrs. Dabbs kept a copy of the Xeroxed manuscript among her papers. On its covering sheet, she made a note: "Ellen Murray wrote the first page of this manuscript, from which the Xerox was made, from the original manuscript of the diary kept by Miss Towne. After page 1, the entire manuscript is in the hand of Miss Towne who kept it originally in two small composition books." This copy now resides in the Edith M. Dabbs Collection at the

University of South Carolina's Carolingiana Library. The woman who catalogued that collection will not commit to a statement that the handwriting actually belongs to Laura Towne, because she has no other corroborating evidence of Laura's hand. The claim, however, seems reasonable to me, since it comes down through the family of Ellen Murray.

One final question remains. Is this copy different from the others? Yes, it is substantially different. When it is side-by-side with the print edition, there are six or seven differences per page. Most of the changes, however, are editorial ones. It is easy to believe that Laura made this copy for her dearest friend, sometimes leaving out small things that Ellen would already know, but more often polishing the language. And here's the telling difference: the disparaging comments about the freedmen from the other copies have been modified or eliminated. It is exactly the sort of editing I can imagine myself doing on something I wrote thirty years ago. In my novelist's imagination, I see Laura shaking her head at her own foolishness and saying, "Oh for Heaven's sake! I can't believe I ever said that!"

Is the result a truer vision of Laura? I think it is. She undoubtedly came to South Carolina with the same inherent prejudices and preconceptions that almost all the abolitionists shared. They had an idealized view of what the Negro race could become, but little knowledge of the realities of slavery until they met it face to face. As a result, they were horrified by much of what they saw. Laura's intemperate reactions in her first weeks there come from that shocking reality. But unlike many of the original abolitionists, who simply gave up and went home, Laura stayed in South Carolina for forty years, working among the people she had come to love.

This handwritten version of her diary speaks to me as none of the other copies do. And I think it gives a clearer picture of the mature Laura than any other source I have found. Laura Towne is not the derogatory words she wrote in her first few days on St. Helena Island. She is, rather, the work she accomplished, the task to which she devoted her entire life. If she edited the diary to reflect the attitudes of a lifetime, that was her privilege. She deserves to be judged by what she did, not by what she said.

~∘~

What a Difference a Date Makes

Shortly after posting my evaluations of the last two diary sources, I made a small, but amazingly significant, discovery. I was leafing through the handwritten copy of Laura Towne's diary, looking for a particular comment, when a date discrepancy caught my eye. One entry was dated "July 19th 1862." The next one was "July 20th 1901" Then came "July 21st 1901" and then "July 22d 1862".

I recognize an obvious explanation here. The person making the copy simply wrote down the current year instead of 1862. I've made the same mistake myself. When you are writing dates, it is all too easy to write down the current year instead of the appropriate one. History students do it on exams all the time, and their professors get a chuckle out of reading that Attila the Hun died in 1998. We've all misdated checks, particularly at the beginning of a new year. I've seen a Jeopardy contestant or two make the same mistake—one that cost them hundreds of dollars.

Now a history student may simply not know the right answer. And a Jeopardy contestant may be guessing. But this is not the same sort of wrong answer. When the wrong date slips out for something you know well, it almost always is a date that has some other significance. In this case, I think it is pretty conclusive evidence that the diary was being copied in 1901. That makes this version the earliest copy of the four, the only one of the four known to the two people who were most involved with it—Laura and Ellen.

But 1901! That's the year that Laura died—on February 20th, if I remember correctly. And that makes it even more important. Here's what I think happened. When the twentieth century dawned, Laura Towne was 75 years old. She was undoubtedly already ill, and, because of her extensive medical training, I am equally sure that she knew she was suffering from a potentially fatal illness. She would have begun putting her affairs in order, and one of the things she wanted to do was make a copy of the diary for her dear friend, Ellen Murray, to keep.

She shortened some of the entries and omitted others. She corrected her intemperate judgments as she went along. She was, in fact, composing her own obituary—writing out the story of her life as she wanted it to be known. And she may not have been able to finish the task. The handwritten copy ends on May 28, 1864. The original diary could have continued much longer.

Does this simple mistaken date prove that Laura herself wrote the copy? No, probably not. Ellen could have done it in the months after Laura died. But it increases the probability that the handwriting is, indeed, Laura's. Once again, I am brought back to Paul Hyams' bit of advice: "Saying 'There is no evidence' is a historian's excuse, not a defense for a novelist. A novelist must bring imagination to the mix, hoping to come up with the hidden solution."

A good friend suggested to me that this whole problem might make a good presentation at a history conference. It would not. Historians do not accept what they cannot prove. But a novelist? A novelist must listen to all those little voices that suggest "what might have been." To my own surprise, I was now hearing the voice of Laura Towne in a way I had not heard her in all the months I had been reading about her. This handwritten copy of her diary now sits on my desk as a personal message, and her words guide and color the story I am trying to tell.

9. Choose Quality over Quantity

Every so often, I receive a reminder that another National Novel Writing Month is approaching. The idea behind NaNoWriMo is speedwriting, or, as some have called it, writing by the seat of your pants. It means sitting down for thirty days in a row and writing something—anything—that pops into your head. You are not supposed to plan ahead or stop to correct any mistakes. You plow along until you have accumulated 50,000 words, which might, or might not, eventually become a novel. Every reminder brings back memories of my two attempts at the November exercise in speedwriting. I thought I might re-cap those two writing adventures to remind myself and other readers of the struggles it takes to write a good book.

❧

Now It's Finished; Now It's Not

I'm now far enough away from my first year of National Novel Writing Month to look back on the experience without feeling stressed out. For those of you who are unfamiliar with this exercise in self-torture, you must write a 50,000-word novel during month of November. And nobody seems to take into account the fact that there's a major holiday right there at the end of the drill. Just plop the turkey in the oven and head back to the keyboard!

In 2009, I made it. Actually, I finished two days ahead of schedule, which should have made me feel good about myself. But if I'm being honest, I have to admit I was not brave enough to go back and see what I wrote. Oh, I violated the rules left and right. They are not designed for an old English teacher who cannot stand to see a spelling error and let it pass. I also backed up to correct silly details like whether a period belonged inside or outside a closing quotation mark. I was pretty confident that what I produced was in passable English. But did it make sense? That was a whole different question.

My 50,000 words (50,626 to be exact) were the finishing chapters of a much longer novel that had been stalled in the middle. After letting it sit there for six months, I signed up for NaNoWriMo, which forced me to jump in and finish the darn thing. I'd been feeling pretty smug ever since I completed the NaNoWriMo competition. The 50,000 words I wrote there nicely finished off my historical novel. I thought all I had left to do was polish it up a bit. Hah!

I had been working on *Beyond All Price*, the life story of a woman by the name of Nellie Chase, who had an amazing experience as a Civil War nurse. Her story is compelling. She was a teenage runaway, the wife of a musician who turned out to be "a drunkard, a liar, a gambler, a forger, and a thief." She escaped from his degrading lifestyle by signing up as a nurse with a Union regiment and traveling with them for a year. During that year she faced the usual hardships, compounded by a vengeful Presbyterian chaplain who thought she was a prostitute and by challenges to her understanding of what it would mean to put an end to slavery.

For that year, I had abundant information in the form of letters from the members of the regiment, all of whom found her interesting enough to talk about at length. But I didn't know who Nellie really was, or what happened to her after the war. That lack of information led me to turn her story into a novel, rather than a biography, and I had great fun creating a life for her before and after the war. NaNoWriMo was perfect for me. I had let my imagination fly and had created an exciting and plausible end to the story. So far so good!

Then one night I received an e-mail from someone else who is interested in the same regiment. He had found two small tidbits of information about Nellie. One letter suggested that she was related to a prominent national figure. The other was an obituary that listed the man she married after the war and told of her heroic death during the Yellow Fever epidemic. My "exciting and plausible" ending was nowhere near as good as the real story. This was definitely a case of the truth being stranger than fiction.

It also meant that I had to discard much of what I wrote in November, as well as segments throughout the rest of the book. Back to the records I went, armed with a new set of names and dates to be checked. It's a good thing I enjoy historical research. The historian in me was excited; the writer, a bit discouraged.

∞◦◦∞

True Confessions

So how did my 2010 venture into National Novel Writing Month turn out? Well, here's what I wrote about it at the beginning of the process:

"The NaNoWriMo process is easier this year. I find I'm better able to sit down and let the words flow. What's developing on my computer screen is by no means a finished product, but it's going to serve as a great base from which to build a real novel. I won't promise you that "Gideon's Ladies" will write itself in the next month. Truth is, I'll still be reading and researching much of the time. I find it easiest to write dialogue, so I'll be concentrating in creating scenes from various spots in the story. They can always be rearranged and polished later. As I write, I'm getting a feel for the characters, and I find that some of the individuals have begun to speak in their own voices, which is always a delightful turning point. I'm anxious now to find out what they are going to do next, and how they will handle the problems they have set for themselves."

By the end of the month, I sounded exhausted and not so sure of what I had managed to accomplish:

"Finished! Yes, that's right! After 27 grueling days (actually 25 work days and 2 days of utter slackerness) I have managed to write the first 50,417 words of my next novel, tentatively entitled "Gideon's Ladies." Was it worth it? Well, sometime after today, I'll realize that it was. The writing phase is always hard, and putting a word counter on every morsel you manage to crank out is a definition of cruelty. But now I know that this story has legs. It can someday become a novel, and when that day comes, I'll be delighted that I spent November 2010 in this effort. For now, however, it's off to start Christmas preparations (and a good stiff drink, too.)"

And now it's true confession time. Although I dutifully sent my "winning" 50,000 words off to CreateSpace—to take them up on their offer to produce a proof copy of every book that qualified at the end of the month—I couldn't bear to look at it in the new year. The thin little volume arrived—some 178 pages in all. But it looked pitiful. It was full of typos and half-finished pages, with thoughts that started off bravely and went absolutely nowhere.

When I finally began re-reading "Gideon's Ladies," I was embarrassed by the number of typos and the layout. Once in a while I was pleased with a particular turn of phrase, but more often I cringed. I have, however, learned a bit more about myself and about the writing process. Here are five rules I would now be willing to carve on a stone:

- Don't start writing until you have some idea of where you're heading. These little chapters utterly fail to provide direction. An impartial reader cannot tell who the important characters are, or what the book is all about.
- Have a timeline. My events are confusingly out of order.
- Don't confuse "show and tell." My academic background reveals itself clearly when I fall into a class lecture mode. I thought I was writing conversations, but the result all too often sounds like a typical schoolmarm *telling* a class of students what they must know for the test. I wrote so quickly

that I forgot to let my characters *show* what was going on through their words and actions.

- Know your characters. Each one needs a distinct personality, recognizable in both their actions and in their speech patterns. If the reader can't tell the characters apart, the author has failed again.
- Write because you have something important to say. The reader deserves to understand what is important about your story and why you care.

So where did I go from there? I had already made a start by changing my title from "Gideon's Ladies" (too over-used) to *The Road to Frogmore*. And that title reflected one other decision—to make Laura Towne and her efforts to establish her own school at Frogmore Plantation the center of my story. My research efforts for the next several weeks focused on obeying my other new rules. I filled out my character sketches, pinpointing those traits that made each character an individual. I finished the timeline I had started, so that the events of my story were both logical and historically accurate. Then I could re-arrange and refurbish some of the chapters I had written. Most important, I needed to make some decisions about point-of-view and recurring themes.

⟳

One More NaNoWriMo Failure

The good folks who bring us National Novel Writing Month (NaNoWriMo) every November expanded their efforts in 2011 to include two months of summer camp. And even though I had vowed never again to try one of these writing marathons, I was drawn in by the novelties they introduced. Participants were egged on by campfires and roasted marshmallows (who can resist a s'more?), and by the second month, we had cabins and cabin mates to encourage us and keep us plugging away. But did it work? Not for me, I'm afraid.

In July, I managed 38,000 words of re-writing the previous year's drivel and turning it into a real shot at my next novel,

The Road to Frogmore. I really thought I could knock out all the required 50,000 words, which would have put me halfway home. Then somehow life got in the way. Maybe it was because my inner English teacher kept getting in the way. Try as I might, I could not write without reading what I had written. I stopped to check the slant of my curly quotes, look up my precise dates and places, and correct every spelling error I saw. Not the way to meet a deadline, but at least the 38,000 words I had were pretty good.

So on I went into August, with six new cabin mates, who all seemed to be working on fantasy, while I was trying to be historical—not the best combination. This time, I faltered at the beginning of the month, missing at least 13 straight days of writing anything (other than blog posts, that is.). As my cabin mates began to fall along the trail, I went back to work. But on the last day of August, I woke up realizing that the month was over, and once again, I was way off the mark at slightly over 24,000 words. Only one person in my cabin actually finished. I came in number three out of seven—pretty mediocre.

Part of the problem was a new computer with a wireless keyboard and touchpad. They were both enough smaller than the old ones to cause massive "fat-fingering" when I tried to touch-type. I was starting to get the hang of it, but I was still missing the "t" key most of the time, which gave my sentences three or four errors for every ten words. Sigh!

As for the other explanations? I'm not convinced that speedwriting is a good idea. Just as I find it difficult to outline my entire plot in advance (because my characters keep changing the story on me!), so I need to vegetate between chapters—to let the ideas brew and the characters speak. It's time to admit that I am not a "seat-of-the-pants" writer.

As for NaNoWriMo, I did not participate in 2011. Speedwriting is a wonderfully useful exercise. It gets the creative juices flowing, and it reveals (make that "painfully" reveals) what kind of writer you are. It's a great start for those who question their own ability to write a book. It does not, however, produce a finished product. The sense of accomplishment it touts is basically flawed. There is simply no substitute for the long, hard process of producing a book good enough to justify its readers' time and interest. For me, the warm-ups were now over. It was time to get to work.

10. Know Where the Story is Headed

The story of the Gideonites and the Port Royal Experiment has no lack of colorful characters. It's full of fascinating people. It has all kinds of exotic scenery—swamps, pluff mud, tropical vegetation, glorious sunrises, sandy ocean beaches. It has drama—a background of America's Civil War, heroic acts of bravery, enormous pain and suffering, and a life-changing struggle for freedom. Why, then, couldn't I make any progress with the book? The answer is right here, in this paragraph. The story was simply too big to handle.

∽౨౿∾

Author Goes on Murderous Rampage

But, oh, how hard it is to cut out all those great tidbits. I had what amounted to half a book already written—some 50,000 words I had created during last year's National Novel Writing Month. The chapters were sitting there, waiting, but I couldn't tell where they were going next. I started cutting hunks out of those chapters, but while the remaining 35,000 words were more coherent, their direction was still unclear.

Eventually, of course, I recognized my own errors. I was writing like a historian. Now, there's nothing wrong with being a historian.

It's what I am by training and experience. I want to know exactly what happened, why it happened, who all was involved, when and where it happened (all the usual journalist's questions), as well as what were the underlying causes and results. All legitimate questions. All important. All calling for more research. And nothing, nothing, that has much to do with the nature of a novel.

The light clicked on while I was reading an article on creating a press release. "Summarize your plot in a single sentence. Then expand it to two sentences. Make the reader want to know what's going to happen." I couldn't do it—because I didn't really have a plot. I was describing events, hoping that they would magically arrange themselves into an acceptable story. So far, they weren't showing any signs of being able to do that on their own. I had 35,000 words, but they weren't the beginning of a novel.

For a novel, I had to build a plot, one with a clear beginning, a middle, and an end. It needed a theme, a message, a reason for its existence. It needed one main character—someone with back story, a character with an appealing personality but a few inner quirks, a character with whom the reader could identify. That character needed a goal that was important not only to her but to the reader, and she needed an adversary that stood in the way of her reaching that goal. The story needed tension, a crisis (or two or three), and a resolution that would be not necessarily happy but reasonable in the light of all that went before.

The solution was obvious but too drastic to contemplate. Instead of trashing the project, I stepped away from it for a while and sought my own guru—someone who could tell me what to do to salvage the idea. I had finished reading a wonderful book: *Story Engineering* by Larry Brooks. He offers a step-by-step guide for building the underlying structure of a novel. As I read, I kept a notepad at hand, where I scratched out ideas of how I could take my historical knowledge and mold it into a workable plot outline. And suddenly my story did arrange itself. Once I had the main structural elements in place, the people, the places, and the events made sense. The 35,000 words? Trashed! The concept of the book? Rejuvenated!

∽○∾

Killing My Darlings

First came the answers to some vital questions:

Q: *Who is the main character?*

A: Laura Matilda Towne is a thirty-something, single, Unitarian, abolitionist medical student in Philadelphia.

Q: *What is her goal?*

A: To prove the validity of the abolitionist belief—that if slavery is abolished, the former slaves can become loyal and productive citizens of the United States—by joining a band of teachers and missionaries known as the Gideonites.

Q: *What obstacles (adversaries) stand in her way?*

A. Her loyalty to family, unfinished medical studies, lack of governmental support for the idea of emancipation, and the multiple dangers of South Carolina in the middle of the Civil War, among others.

Q: *What's my "elevator pitch"?*

A: Laura Towne abandons family, friends and career plans to travel to South Carolina in the middle of the Civil War to help prove that freed slaves can become loyal and productive citizens.

Next came a close scrutiny of my cast of characters. And here's where I had to launch into mayhem and murderous rampage. When I listed all the names of real people with whom Laura came in contact during her first years in South Carolina, there turned out to be hundreds of them—and most of those had to go. I examined both individuals and groups, always asking the same question: *Did this person help or hinder Laura in a significant way?* If the answer was yes, the character stayed. But if I could not make a case for individuals as significant, I killed their characters, no matter how fascinating their personal stories seemed.

The members of the Roundhead Regiment, including Nellie Chase and her small family of ex-slaves, were some of my favorite, but unnecessary, characters. True, they were in Beaufort when

Laura arrived. They met on several occasions. Laura and Nellie had a few similar slave encounters. But there is no evidence that Nellie influenced Laura in any way. That they reached somewhat similar conclusions speaks only to the validity of those conclusions. Although I have had readers of A *Scratch with the Rebels* and *Beyond All Price* ask for more, these characters have already had their moments in the sun. This new book was not their story.

Robert Smalls lived an amazing life for a slave. He had a connection with Laura's group of Gideonites because his wife and children lived at Coffin Point, the plantation run by Edward Philbrick. Laura visited often, bringing medical care to the freedmen there, and when Smalls pulled off his great act of derring-do, I'm sure Laura was among those who cheered him. But while others of the Gideonites hustled Smalls off to Washington to show that a slave could do great things for the country, his accomplishments had no permanent effect on Laura or the children in Laura's classroom. This was not his story, either.

Harriet Tubman was a plucky little slave woman from Maryland, who led escaped slaves along the Underground Railroad, penetrated Confederate lines to spy for the United States, and led a raid into the interior of South Carolina to rescue slaves and bring them to safety in the Low Country. Laura knew her and admired her. Harriet certainly made an impact on St. Helena Island when she turned up leading over 700 newly freed slaves, hoping that someone would house them, feed them, and teach them what they needed to know. But did her actions influence Laura and her ability to achieve her goal? Not really. Harriet Tubman deserves her own books. This was not one of them.

The Gideonites were a fascinating group of people. A total of seventy-three northerners traveled to South Carolina in the spring of 1862, all determined in one way or another to prove the rightness of the abolitionist cause. They were socialites and sheltered spinsters, old and young, teachers, ministers, lawyers, philanthropists, and failed businessmen. And they all had back stories that explained why they gave up everything to risk this venture. How could I ignore the spiritual leader of the group who found himself on trial as a kleptomaniac? The opera singer with seven children who wrote such lurid prose that she could almost be classified as a pornographer? The cotton agent who beat one of the other Gideonites to a battered and bloody wreck? The wealthy socialite who could not lower herself to do actual work of any kind? The free black woman who confounded everyone who expected to see a clear color separation between teachers and students by being both teacher and black?

The Gideonites as a group are worthy of study, and as individuals their stories make great reading. Once again, my reasons for choosing to feature some of them and ignore others depended on the impact they had on Laura and her goal. If they played a crucial role in the plot, they stayed. If they went home early or had nothing to contribute to the main story, I excluded them.

The former slaves themselves were vital to the story. There were hundreds of them, and without them, Laura's reason for being in South Carolina disappeared. Each of them had a tale to tell, as Austa, the pornographer, discovered. But to focus on each one of them would be impossible. Instead I chose to let one strong woman, Laura's laundress, speak for all of them. Rina was present for the whole story. In the final version of the book, she will comment on events and tell the stories that the others cannot pass on. Think of her as a one-woman black chorus, speaking for all of those who were once enslaved.

꙳Ꙩꙩ꙳

Character Sketches

Even after my murderous rampage, I still had a fascinating cast of characters as ingredients in the brew that would eventually become a novel. In 1861, a group of abolitionists from Boston, New York, and Philadelphia set sail for coastal South Carolina. Word had arrived of a great Union victory at Port Royal Sound. The Confederate inhabitants had been driven out of the coastal islands, which had been full of cotton and tea plantations. White slave owners grabbed what they could carry and fled into the interior. Their slaves found themselves abandoned, and, to all intents and purposes, free. The abolitionists hoped to offer their aid to these ex-slaves. They brought food supplies, used clothing, books, Bibles, and the own eagerness to prove that slaves could be turned into productive citizens.

The remaining missionaries were still a motley group. One of their fellow passengers aboard the ship that carried them described them thus: "bearded and mustached and odd-looking men, with odder-looking women." Another suggested that they were "broken-down schoolmasters or ministers who have excellent dispositions but not much talent." Such quirks meant that they were going to be fun to work with. But my first problem was getting to know them as individuals, so that my readers could tell them apart.

This is where I learned that compiling a character sketch of each person is an indispensable first step. To my delight, I discovered that the new version of "Scrivener" provides a template for such sketches. The template offers the following sections: role in story, occupation, physical description, personality, habits and mannerisms, background, internal conflicts, external conflicts and notes. Here are some of the resources I used to compile this information for my works of historical fiction.

Since most of my characters were real people, I started with a general history text that described the events I wanted to write about. Plundering the index was a quick way to locate my characters and identify such details as occupation and background.

My second resource was the U. S. Census. Any good genealogy program can quickly locate any mention of the character in whom you are interested. I've been concentrating on such things as the family's economic status and my individual's place within the family. Among the women, I found one who was the only girl in a huge family of boys—thus explaining, perhaps, why so many people commented on her masculine habits. Another was a nine-year-old-child when her mother died, leaving her to help raise four younger brothers and sisters. No need to wonder where she developed her nurturing nature.

Photographs can reveal much. One of my ladies was a spinster, uniformly adored by the children she taught but an object of scorn to many of the men around her. Why? Well, a single glance at her only formal portrait draws attention her unfortunately huge bulbous nose.

The character's own writings—letters, diaries, journals, other publications—complete the picture. One of my characters was a preacher's wife. I knew she was a singer and a teacher, as well as the leading force among the evangelical abolitionists. I didn't fully understand her, however, until I discovered a book she had written about the evils of slavery. It shows her not only as an intemperate zealot, but as a lascivious one at that. I might have missed that part of her character if I had not taken the time to compile a character sketch.

The template works equally well for fantasy, purely fictional characters, historical figures, and even the people involved in historical monographs. You must know your character well before you can expect your reader to understand and identify with him.

◌◌◌

Speed-Date Your Characters

Most writing handbooks will provide a useful list of rules for creating characters. Make the people in your novel believable. Avoid stereotypes, which are, by definition, boring. Reveal personalities a bit at a time. Let the reader get to know your characters gradually, in much the same way as you get to know real people in your life. But how do you do all that?

One way is to imagine your characters in a speed-dating setting. Visualize each one sitting across from you. You have only a few minutes to decide if you like or distrust them. Besides noting the usual hair and eye color, height and weight, ask each of them a series of questions:

- What is your name? Does it have a special significance to your family? Do you have a nickname?
- How old are you, and where were you born? Have you stayed in one location or moved around? And if you have moved, at what point in your life?
- What was your family like when you were growing up? Did you have brothers and sisters, and where do you fall, age-wise, in the list of your parents' children? Are you still the responsible one because you were the oldest? Or are you the forgotten middle child, or the spoiled youngest one?
- Did you have pets as a child? If you could choose just one pet, would you turn out to be a cat-person (independent) or a dog-person (eager and friendly)?
- Do you have a large circle of companions, or only a couple of close friends? Have you moved in the same small circle all your life, or have you reached out to meet new people? And how do you choose your friends?
- What is your greatest strength? Your greatest weakness?
- What do you dream of doing? If you could be someone else, who would you choose?
- What beliefs do you hold most tightly? Which ones would you be willing to carve on a rock?
- What is your idea of a perfect day? Where and with whom would you spend it, and what would you do?
- Why do you dress the way you do? Are you usually neat or disheveled? Are you stylish or old-fashioned? Are you uncomfortable in a suit and tie—or in high heels and a fancy dress?
- What are your favorite expressions? Do you use the latest slang, or do you show off your extensive vocabulary? Do you slip into a more pronounced accent or dialect when you are excited? Do you have a verbal tic, saying "um" or "uh" or "like" or "you know"?
- What does your posture say about you? Do you slouch, or hunch your shoulders, or keep your arms crossed? Do

you keep your eyes on the ground when you walk? Or are your shoulders thrown back as a sign of confidence?

- What about eye contact? Do you keep looking away, or are you giving me a belligerent stare? Are you squinting at me or raising a skeptical eyebrow? Are you avoiding eye contact because you are nervous or because you are bored? Does your smile reach your eyes?
- Does standing close to someone make you uncomfortable? Or do you frequently reach out to make physical contact?
- And what do your other gestures say about you? Do you play with your hair or brush it back impatiently? Do you have a "twitch" or unconscious mannerism? Do you pick at a hangnail, chew your lip, shuffle your feet, or bite your fingernails?

We all send out signals with our body language, and most of us are able to interpret those signals, if only subconsciously. If your characters behave as real people do, your readers will judge them accordingly.

ᪧ

Mapping Your Way through Time

I've learned that any time I spend figuring out the details of chronology at the beginning of a writing project saves me many more hours of time down the line. In historical fiction, chronology is vital. Without a thorough command of historical events, a seat-of-the-pants author runs the risk of including modern opinions in the attitudes of old-fashioned people, misdating known events, or (horrors of horrors!) having a long-dead character suddenly reappear later in the book. I use timelines to avoid such problems.

In a recent book, a timeline became increasingly important when I realized how many sources of information I had, and how great was the potential for them to contradict each other. I desperately needed a chronology of the Civil War itself. I was referring to government documents, which frequently postdated the events they were reporting. I had a massive historical work that recounted the activities of the Port Royal Experiment, well documented but not always well dated. Footnotes referring to actions tended to record when the report was made, not when the event occurred. And finally came several volumes of personal letters and diaries, each of which had a slightly different slant. Add to all of that the problem of relatives who had censored the letters and diaries. The potential for disaster was enormous.

Here's how I approached the challenge. I use timeline creation software for MAC called, appropriately, Timeline 3D. It allows all sorts of variations and creative designs. For each event, you can add a title, a date, a photo, and an explanatory sentence or two. I started with a standard list of the most important events of the Civil War—battles, major troop movements, elections, and acts of Congress.

To clarify the major problems presented by the heavily edited Laura Towne materials, I set up a different timeline. This time, I listed every letter or diary entry that I could find. I used a different font for each version for the material, so that the censored material would stand out from that of the published versions.

Finally, I created an "Export" version of each file and then pasted the resulting texts into a standard Excel worksheet, one after the other. By then I was looking at some nine pages of single-spaced entries. Running a "Sort A to Z" operation on the file combined the lists and rearranged all the entries into one chronological file. After that, I could sort out the important events and begin to see a basic outline of the book-to-be.

There are, of course, many other ways to approach this problem, and other software companies to provide the tools. What really matters is that you take the time to discover what happened, and in what order. Then it becomes easy to identify the arcs of your story—the dominant goal, the crisis points, and the resolution. Time(lines) well spent!

11. Clarify Points of View and Themes

You can't figure out how to get to where you're going until you know where you are. That may sound like a formula for a travel column, but it applies equally well to the design of a book. It also applies to the writer and to the reader. It's called establishing a point of view. If the writer has not decided on a point of view, the resulting book will wander around from character to character without focus. And if the reader cannot recognize the point of view, the story will make little sense.

∽◦∾

Does Anyone Have a Program?

There are actually five points of view from which to choose:

- First-person—classic "I" narrative, with writer speaking as main character.
- Second-person—"You" approach, which tries to convince the reader that he is the main character. That one's hard to pull off unless you're writing a how-to book.
- Limited Third-person—in which the author reveals only the reactions or experiences of the main character. The reader sees everyone's spoken words, but knows only what the main character is feeling and thinking.

- Third-person-omniscient—The author views the story from above, and knows what is going on in everyone's mind. If there are many characters in a story, there may be too much information.
- Mixed-POV—in which the lead character dominates the narrataive, while separate chapters in third-person reveal what else is happening.

I had been puzzling over point of view for weeks. When I wrote my 50,000 words of "Gideon's Ladies" for National Novel Writing Month" (NaNoWriMo), I typed away, without ever considering point of view. The result was a mish mash. Each day's output had a slightly different focus, and a second reading revealed that I had no idea where I was going.

The story of the Port Royal missionaries is, of course, a mish mash in itself. People come and go. Leadership changes. The events of the Civil War affect what is happening in the Low Country with unexpected results. The missionaries become involved in one dispute after another, and their alliances change with every change in the political winds that blow through their affairs.

I began to understand the magnitude of the problem when I tried to use Randy Ingermanson's "Snowflake Pro" software to outline my novel. It's a 10-step program, and I only made it to step two before I knew I was lost. Step Two asked for a one-paragraph synopsis of the story: the set-up, the disasters that occur, and the ending. Sounds simple, right? Hah! Story takes place in South Carolina during the Civil War. OK. That's the set-up. So far, so good.

Now for disasters. Those we have in abundance. Storms, raids, murders, boll weevils, smallpox, yellow fever, vandalism, fistfights, searing heat, killing frosts, hangings, invasions, battles, conflicting laws, drownings—the list goes on and on. But whose disasters are they? The emancipation proclamation is a disaster for the cotton agent whose workers walk off the job to celebrate their freedom. A threat of invasion is a disaster for the missionaries whose sponsors call them home, but it's a victory for the plantation owner who sees the slave schools close and his field hands come back to work. The failure of a cotton crop because of worm infestation is a disaster for the cotton farmer but a blessing for the field hand, who can now devote full time to the crops that will feed his family through the winter. The missionary-teachers celebrate the firing of a corrupt cotton agent, who must return home in disgrace. The cotton agents smile when they see a prominent minister recalled for lining his own pockets with money that should have gone to the plantations. It all depends on point of view.

I began to find my way when I started asking the right questions. Whose story is this? Who is most affected by the events? Who has the most to lose?

∽‿૯‿૭

Whose Story Is this, Anyway?

Whose story is being told in *The Road to Frogmore*? Who is most affected by the events? Who has the most to lose? I thought I knew that my focus would fall on Laura Towne, the founder of the Penn Center, but she was not yet in the area when some of the crucial events took place. In almost every case, the slaves were the ones whose lives were being turned upside down. But could I write the story from the slaves' point of view? That would be a real stretch, for a couple of reasons.

First, there is almost no evidence of what the slaves thought about the goings-on in the Low Country during the Civil War. It would be accurate to say they were confused, I suppose, but there is no actual evidence to back up even that claim. Because it was against state law to teach a slave to read or write, there are no letters or diaries. Most of the slaves spoke the Gullah language among themselves. The first whites who came to work with them found them almost unintelligible. With no record of what they thought, I would be unwilling to trust my creative ability to fictionalize their attitudes.

Second, the slaves were not in a position to understand much of what was going on around them. Even if we could find some record of their reactions, they were limited because no one had ever told them about politics, or military strategy, or religious differences. Some of them had heard about Baby Jesus and Uncle Sam, but they had no real understanding of those concepts. Their white masters had wanted them kept as ignorant as possible because a lack of knowledge kept them from rising up in revolt. No, the slaves would not do as the narrators of my story.

And yet, I needed their point of view! As I struggled to deal with this issue, I realized that I did have a bit of evidence about the slaves after all. In the Laura Towne diary and letters, Laura made repeated references to Rina, the woman who did her laundry and ironing for a small salary. Rina held an important place in the slave matriarchy, evidenced by the fact that when the slaves assembled for a "Shout," they did so at Rina's cabin. Laura, too, found that Rina was invaluable. The diary echoes with one phrase—"Rina tells me that. . . ." As trust built up between the two women, Rina became Laura's window into the world of the slaves. Rina also functioned as something of a one-woman Greek chorus, commenting on the events of the day and the foolishness of the white people around her.

Once I understood Rina's role in my story, the point-of-view decision became clear. This book will use a mixed point of view, except for the sections devoted to Rina. Rina's comments and stories will appear in short chapters written in first person. Laura's diary provides a close enough approximation to allow me to record Rina's own words, and I must let her speak for herself. But she cannot speak about all the ideological differences that erupt into crisis points in the story. Since she does not understand what the cotton agents are trying to accomplish, their part of the story must appear in a third-person narrative. The same is true of the soldiers and of the missionaries who come to South Carolina from a variety of backgrounds and with diverse motives.

When Rina speaks, she knows only what her own experiences have taught her. She may make assumptions about the other characters, but she will be presenting a single opinion that is already formed. She speaks her mind, allowing the reader to understand her, even if the truths she speaks are unwelcome. When the book turns to the people who surround Rina, the third person point of view allows the reader to form his own opinion about each of the characters because it offers many views.

Because there are so many stories to be told, I may try to use a mixed third-person point of view for all of the characters except Rina. Each chapter will clearly designate the character who appears as the subject of that chapter. Switching the point of view will allow the reader to relate to one character at a time as the focus shifts to those who are most affected by events at any given time. The result, I hope, will allow the reader a clearer understanding of what the Gideonite Experiment was all about.

And that, I think, will be the real message of the book. It will present as dispassionately as possible the ideological clashes that make up the great divide during the Civil War. It will not choose between North and South, Evangelical and Unitarian, abolitionist and slave owner, civilian and soldier, businessman and humanitarian, states rights advocate and federalist. But the one constant feature will be the voice of Rina, reminding the reader that she is the one with the most to lose if the world makes the wrong choices.

∞◡◠◠

An Irish Puzzlement

On St. Patrick's Day, everyone wants to be thought of as at least part-Irish. It makes a wonderful reason to go out for a pint of Guinness or some corned beef and cabbage. Irish brogues and Irish blessings seem to be on everyone's tongue. Green clothes emerge from the backs of closets, and if you don't wear green on that day, you can expect to be pinched by one of those celebrants who may have imbibed a bit too heavily of green beer. This was not always the case, however.

I am reminded how frequently various nationalities have suffered from discrimination because they seemed strange or different, and the Irish were no exception. One hundred and fifty

113

years ago, it was the Irish who were regarded by many Americans as somewhat inferior forms of humanity. That form of prejudice leaps out at me as I read about the abolitionist attempts to prove that the children of southern slaves were as capable as white children of getting an education.

Here's one example, taken from letter written by Edward Philbrick, a Gideonite missionary in South Carolina. He had been telling his wife why he believed newly freed slaves were fully capable of becoming useful citizens. He says, "Think of their having reorganized and gone deliberately to work here some weeks ago, without a white man near them, preparing hundreds of acres for the new crop. The Irish wouldn't have done as much in the same position." Another of the missionaries commented that to one who was used to seeing the stupidity of Irish faces, the slaves did not appear to "suggest a new idea of low humanity."

There seems to be an underlying assumption in the thinking of the Civil War period that some people are naturally inferior to others. Several of the missionaries speak of the Irish as one of the "degraded races" of people who had fallen from their original state of natural equality to a lesser status. I've been shocked to see that the same people who argue for the inherent ability of the former slaves have no qualms about sneering at the inferiority of the Irish. As a counterbalance, it is also easy to find the Bostonian Irish making the same disparaging remarks about Negroes in general, perhaps because they saw them as competition in the labor force.

This attitude will play a central role in my story, I think.

ᏬᏋᎧ

A Problem in Semantics

The northern abolitionists who traveled to South Carolina during America's Civil War, ostensibly to help the newly freed slaves, all agreed that the institution of slavery was wrong and that the slaves had to be given their freedom. They were less clear about what they meant by "freedom." A few believed that the slaves only needed to be set free; what they did after that was up to them. Others understood that people who had been slaves their entire lives would need to be taught how to be free. Some meant economic freedom; some meant religious freedom; others meant political freedom.

And if the abolitionists were confused, imagine the poor slaves. In November 1861, a combined Union Army and Navy Expedition had sailed into a vast South Carolina anchorage. They terrifyied the plantation owners who lived along the South Carolina coast. The planters simply grabbed what they could carry and fled to the interior of the state. Almost to a man, they abandoned their slaves to their own resources. The slave reactions were varied, but predictable.

When slave women were told they were "free," the idea frequently sent them into fits of weeping and wailing. To the women, it meant they were being turned out of the only homes they had ever known. Where should they go? What would they do? Who would take care of them?

To the men, particularly the field hands, being free meant no one was going to make them work ever again. They freed themselves from their hoes and their plows and sat down, waiting to see what would happen next—unable to make the leap of understanding that they were still going to have to work if they wanted to eat.

And the youngsters? They took the word free to mean something even more literal. Many of the young men went on a rampage, breaking into the plantation houses to liberate the goods therein. They tore up carpets to make suits, donned clothing left behind by fleeing masters, ate and drank whatever they could find, and smashed the items for which they had no use. For them, freedom meant complete release from all the rules.

In the period I'm writing about, freedom was a particularly difficult concept. The problems it engendered will also become a part of my overarching theme.

∽☙❧∽

The Challenge of the Touchy Subject

The next step in re-designing the new book was to identify the theme or message. What's a theme? Hard to identify! I see two major ideas affecting almost every step of my story. Both of them are controversial.

The first has to do with the abolitionists as a group. They talk easily about the evils of slavery, the need for emancipation, and the potential for turning slaves into loyal and productive citizens. Laura herself agreed with every one of those points. But what the Gideonites don't seem to recognize is the degree to which they harbor some level of prejudice against the blacks. They want the slaves freed but still see them as a working class. They are willing to pay them a small salary for their labor, but they need them to keep working at the same jobs they have always done. They observe the religious practices that go on in the slave cabins—the Shout, for example—and label them heathenish. They complain that the blacks are no longer obedient. They want the slaves to change their child-raising practices, their marriage customs, their level of cleanliness, their manner of dress. They want to free the blacks and then turn them into whites. But they do not really expect them to rise to their own level of personhood.

Laura is as guilty of these attitudes as any of the abolitionists, but she does struggle against them. In several places in her diary, she marvels at incidents in which she forgot the issue of race. Two black schoolteachers visit her one day, and at dinner the conversation is exciting and stimulating as they discuss the methods that work well in the classroom. Later she writes that she enjoyed the evening so much that she failed to notice that the two visitors were black.

What will be the readers' reaction to such incidents? Will they feel uncomfortable about being reminded that even the best of us has inborn prejudices against those who are different? Does the above incident make you think any less of Laura? Are my readers going to see this theme as polemic? I'm assuming that people more or less expect a Civil War novel to deal with racial issues. Of course it must do so, and the revelation that even the staunchest abolitionist was not 100% color blind may not be particularly shocking.

But there is another issue that lies beneath my entire story, one that deals with gender roles. Laura Towne had a friend, Ellen Murray. They were (take your pick): best friends, life-long companions, partners, intimate friends, soulmates. All those terms have been applied to these two women, who left their families and fled to South Carolina to establish their own household and work together toward a common cause. They lived together for forty years, remaining faithful to one another to the exclusion of all others, until death parted them.

I have been unable to find any overt mention of a sexual relationship between the two women, but given the repressive nature of nineteenth-century mores, that is not surprising. Married couples did not often talk about sex in the 1860s, either. But there are intense emotional moments. Laura fears that Ellen will not be able to join her and literally faints with relief when Ellen actually arrives. The two greet each other with restraint and then "cavort with glee" when they are finally alone. Laura is at one spot struck dumb by Ellen's fragile beauty. Ellen believes her purpose in life is to take care of Laura. The crisis points in Laura's story usually have to do with Ellen. Changes in their relationship send their story off in new directions. It is simply impossible to talk about one without talking about both.

The relationship has gone undefined by historians. I suspect that is at least in part because of our own societal disagreements about same-sex marriages and partnerships. In the nineteenth century, there was an accepted family structure known as a "Boston marriage." Even gender studies experts disagree about the exact nature of the relationship, but it always seems to involve two unrelated women living together as husband and wife, thus forming a family unit. Is this what was going on between Laura and Ellen?

Can I ignore it in this book? I don't think I can. I don't want to get into a whole discussion about "otherness" here. However, if Laura and Ellen are a part of a gender-based minority—if they experience discrimination because of their affection for one another—then that may help explain why they choose to build their life together in the isolation of the Sea Islands rather than the urban settings of their upbringings. Their experience may also give them more empathy for the problems faced by the freed slaves, who are also victims of ongoing discrimination.

12. Listen to Your Inner English Teacher

Istarted teaching high school English for the first time when I was barely twenty-one, but the job aged me rapidly. Not that it was hard—the kids were great. But other people? Not so great. I was shocked the first few times I received a strange reaction when my husband introduced me to his friends and colleagues. The conversations would go something like this:

"Hello, I understand you're Lt. Schriber's wife."

"Yes, hi, I'm Carolyn." (big smile, hand extended, eager to please).

"How are you settling in?"

"Just fine, thanks, although we may face some minor bumps when I start work next week." (a little shrug)

"Oh, you work? What do you do?"

"I'm going to be teaching English at (local) High School." (proud and excited to have found a job)

"Oh." (new person makes rapid escape, leaving me standing there feeling abandoned.)

The "Oh" was often followed by one of several responses: *"Excuse me, I'm needed in the kitchen." "I always hated English." "You don't look old enough to be an English teacher." "I thought they were all elderly ladies with warts on their chins. "Oh, dear, now I'll be afraid to talk to you." "You're going to correct my grammar, aren't you?"*

You get the idea. People shied away from me if they were self-conscious about a lack of education, or they shunned me if they had had a bad school experience. I even considered lying about it and saying I was a home economics teacher, until I realized that then no one would ever invite me to dinner. In the 60s, many people feared teachers or actively disliked them. I'd have been much more popular if I had been a shoe clerk.

For that reason, I have been a bit bemused to realize that my most popular blogs are now about the things I used to teach. Maybe I'm hanging out with a better crowd these days. At any rate, the next few chapters offer you a few guidelines that you may find helpful. If you get tired of English class, skip the parts you don't need. I'll make an honest effort not to sound like an elderly lady with warts on my chin.

☙❧

Conquering Commas

Have you ever really tried to understand a grammar book? Most sound like this:

"Commas are punctuation marks with a variety of different uses. They primarily deal with helping the reader identify grammatical relationships between items in a sentence, and are often instrumental in establishing the flow of a sentence. Both commas and semicolons can link independent clauses together, but they're used in different ways. When you use a comma to link two independent clauses together, you also need to use a coordinating conjunction such as "and." The relationship between the two clauses changes slightly based on which coordinating conjunction you use. A semicolon can also link independent clauses, but does not require a coordinating conjunction."

Do rules about how to use commas make you turn purple? No wonder! Let's see if we can make them easier.

Commas are a relatively recent invention. When the Romans first started writing things down, they didn't have punctuation marks. They didn't have spaces for that matter, or lower case letters. SOALLTHEIRWRITINGLOOKEDLIKE

120

THISOBVIOUSLYTHATWASAPROBLEMFORTHEPO
ORGUYWHOHADTOREADIT

Just as spaces showed a reader when one word stopped and another started, so commas told a reader when to pause and take a breath. They were especially welcome when sentences grew longer than "Me hungry. Kill deer."

Try reading this sentence out loud: "At the grocery we bought the following items: peas and carrots and macaroni and cheese and chicken and dumplings."

Obviously you need to replace some of the ands with commas, but which ones? That will depend on how many separate items appeared on the cash register tape. Did you buy peas, carrots, a box of dry macaroni, a package of cheese, a whole chicken, and some frozen dumplings for a total of six items? Or did you buy three: peas and carrots, macaroni and cheese, and chicken and dumplings? Read the two versions aloud and listen for the differences.

Other comma rules apply to things like appositives, direct address, and restrictive versus nonrestrictive clauses. You won't need such esoteric terms if you apply the pause rule. Consider this scenario. A fire occurred in the middle of the night at a rooming house where several men were living. Deaths resulted. How many died?

"The men who were asleep died in the fire." (The sleepers died. The poker-players did not.) "The men, who were asleep, died in the fire." (They were all asleep and they all died.)

Listen for the pauses. Add commas.

As an aside, academics sometimes argue over what is called the Oxford comma. That's the one that appears before the final "and" in a series. When I read a series of terms (like pens, notebooks, pencils, and erasers), I hear a pause after pencils, and I always use the Oxford comma. In other words, I follow my own rule about hearing commas. You may, however, encounter an editor who thinks that extra comma is not only unnecessary but adds an extra expense—one likely to drag the publisher into instant bankruptcy. She will tell you that a comma takes the place of a conjunction, so you never need both. My advice? Don't waste your breath on an argument in which both sides are right. Gracefully bow out, taking your Oxford commas with you. (Because editors always win.)

༄ৎৄ

When Do You Use a Hyphen? And Why?

Hyphens are much less common today than they used to be. In most instances you can probably get away with omitting them entirely. Here are a few exceptions.

Hyphens are used in many compound words to show that the component words have a combined meaning (e.g. a pick-me-up, mother-in-law, good-hearted) or that there is a relationship between the words that make up the compound: for example, rock-forming minerals are minerals that form rocks. But you don't need to use them in every type of compound word.

With compound adjectives formed from the adverb well and a participle (e.g. well-known), or from a phrase (e.g. up-to-date), you should use a hyphen when the compound comes before the noun: "well-known brands of coffee" or "an up-to-date account," but not when the compound comes after the noun: His music was also well known in England. Their figures are up to date.

It's important to use hyphens in compound adjectives describing ages and lengths of time; leaving them out can make the meaning ambiguous. For example, 250-year-old trees clearly refers to trees that are 250 years old, while 250 year old trees could equally refer to 250 trees that are all one year old.

Use a hyphen to separate a prefix from a name or date, e.g. post-Aristotelian or pre-1900.

Use a hyphen to avoid confusion with another word: for example, to distinguish re-cover (= provide something with a new cover) from recover (= get well again).

Hyphens can also be used to divide words that are not usually hyphenated. They show where a word is to be divided at the end of a line of writing. Always try to split the word in a sensible place, so that the first part does not mislead the reader: for example, hel-met not he-lmet; dis-abled not disa-bled.

Hyphens are also used to stand for a common second element in all but the last word of a list. For example, you may see a yield that is two-, three-, or fourfold.

ᏋᎧᏋ

Punctuation Marks We Can Do Without
SEMI-COLONS

Once you've mastered the comma, most English grammar books ask you to consider the semi-colon. Please don't. Semi-colons are pretentious, and they serve no needed function, except in one limited instance. The rule says, when you have two independent clauses (two subjects, two verbs) you can join them with a conjunction or a semi-colon. But only academics use them that way; if you're writing fiction or guidelines that you want to be useful, stick with conjunctions. (There, now. Didn't that sound stuffy?)

Only use a semi-colon in one instance—in a series, in which each item has a qualifying phrase attached loosely to it. Consider this sentence and its variation:

"I invited Eric, the boy in the blue shirt, Emily, a friend who plays the piano, Joshua, a neighbor from down the street, Sam, the kid nobody likes, and Sally." (How many people received an invitation? Nine or five?) If you leave all the commas in, like this, you mean you invited nine people, some of them with names and some with identifying tags.

"I invited Eric, the boy in the blue shirt; Emily, a friend who plays the piano; Joshua, a neighbor from down the street; Sam, the kid nobody likes; and Sally." The punctuation is correct here, but it, too, looks like an English teacher wrote it. (And remember, nobody loves an English teacher.)

When you are tempted to use a semi-colon, take a break from writing. Your readers will thank you for it.
COLONS:

There. I just used one, but you didn't need it to know that the word "colons" was a subject heading, did you? If I could, I would abolish all colons from informal or fiction writing. Why? Because they fail to meet the primary definition of a punctuation mark. Hmmmm? You've forgotten already, haven't you?

Punctuation marks were invented to help oral readers know when to breathe or when to stop talking, or when to raise the tone of the voice at the end of a question. The colon cannot be pronounced, or breathed, or indicated by tone of voice. The only thing it says is "A list is coming." And lists have no business cropping up in fiction. As a writer, you can be much more creative than that.

Now see what we've accomplished? We've eliminated the need for a whole key on the QWERTY keyboard. If I could, I would replace it with a much more useful one—your favorite expletive, for use every time you mistype a word or accidentally delete something important. (I once found a stick-on key with a four-letter word printed on it. It was non-functional, but a great stress-reliever. Before I finished my first book, I had pounded the lettering right off it.)

EXCLAMATION POINTS

We can't do away with these entirely, but like the semi-colon, I recommend that you use them as if they were as expensive as diamonds. One diamond, no matter how small, glitters and looks beautiful. Put a hundred of them in a pile, and they start looking like glass beads. The same thing is true of an exclamation point.

If your character hits his thumb with a hammer, you can write down what he says in one of two ways: "Ouch!"—or—"Ouch," he exclaimed. The punctuation mark is obviously more effective than the verb.

But never do this: Ouch!!!!!!!!!!!!! Now you haven't shown pain or excitement. You've built a picket fence, which will shut your reader off as certainly as a real fence.

AMPERSANDS

Do you even know what one looks like? Or where it came from? (Here's where my medieval training comes in handy.) An ampersand is that funny looking symbol on the 7-key.

&

It originated in a medieval scriptorium, where overworked monks lettered Latin Bibles and charters by hand. Both to speed up their work and to save parchment, which was ridiculously expensive, they created symbols that worked like abbreviations. An ampersand is the Latin word "et" or "and" written with a single swipe of the pen. It's the letter "e" with the tail crossed to form the "t".

Unless you are a native speaker of Latin (in which case you are long-dead) or a monk (in which case you may be hopelessly behind the times), you have no excuse for using it. I vote to send it to the same scrap heap as the colon. Except for one example. Law firms, which tend to be old-fashioned and stuffy themselves, sometimes give themselves a name that they think looks impressive. Featherstone & Higgenbottom may have an important role to play in your novel. But writing, "He bought fish & chips" looks silly and sounds worse. Remember, punctuation tells an oral reader what to do with his voice. Do you really want to say "He bought fish et chips"?

◦◦◦

Spelling—Cna Ouy Rdea Htis?

Studies have demonstrated that most people look at the line above and have no trouble reading it as "Can you read this." Experts think that our minds are conditioned to switch the letters around until they form a recognizable word. That may be so, but fussy folks (like English teachers and other literary types) expect a writer to be able to spell. Nothing will get your manuscript tossed into the trashcan more quickly than having misspelled words—especially if one of then happens to be the name of the agent or publisher you are trying to woo. I really worry about today's teenagers who have grown up knowing "how 2 txt w/ as few ltrs as psbl." We may have raised a whole generation of unemployable illiterates.

Grammar books will offer all sorts of rules, some of which I know you've heard.

- "I before E except after C." This one works sometimes, but it doesn't apply if the word is pronounced with an AY, (neighbor, vein) and there are other inexplicable exceptions (either, foreign).
- "To add an ending to a word that ends with a silent E, drop the E before adding an ending that begins with a vowel, (curve becomes curving), and keep the E if the ending begins with a consonant (wise becomes wisely)." But of course there are exceptions, such as mileage and judgment.
- "When you add an ending to a word that ends with Y, change the Y to I and then add the ending (worry becomes worries)." But the rule does not apply to adding -ING ((worrying) or when the Y is preceded by a vowel (saying).
- Do you want to talk about doubling final consonants? I don't even want to try to find clear examples of this one. The answer is, you do and you don't, depending on the number of syllables in the word and the placement of the accent. Don't ask. Look it up.

Now, it would be nice if I could offer you some easy rules, comparable to the comma rule, to get you past this problem. Surely, phonics instructors and *Sesame Street* taught us how to pronounce our letters. But the English language, being terribly English at times, does not lend itself to rules. Do you doubt that? Then think of these words and say them out loud: doubt, although, through, cough, rough, drought, dough, ought. Tell me now, how do you pronounce the following letter combination: **OUGH** ?

Here are the only rules I think you can trust. Use the spell-checker on your computer constantly, but don't rely on it to catch every spelling error. It won't catch the difference between too, to, and two, for example, or any other pair of words that sound alike.

Buy a good (new!) dictionary and check it whenever you are in doubt. Remember that the meanings of words change over time, old words become obsolete, and new ideas and new technologies spawn whole new vocabularies. Don't try to sound sophisticated by using English spelling for words like centre or colour. They make you sound like you made a wrong turn somewhere in the middle of the Atlantic Ocean. (But if your publishing company happens to be located in England, all bets are off.)

13. Listen to What You Say

Life is unfair. Those who want to be comedians have a difficult time being funny. Those who are trying to write something serious often end up being unintentionally hilarious. Assuming that you do not want your readers to laugh at you instead of with you, I thought I'd offer you some examples of how not to write.

∽⊙∾

Don't Let Your Modifiers Dangle
Consider the picture painted by the following sentences:
- Having been thrown in the air, the dog caught the stick.
- Smashed flat by a passing truck, Rover sniffed at what was left of a half-eaten hamburger.
- The young girl was walking the dog in a short skirt.
- The dog was chasing the boy with the spiked collar.
- Piled up next to the washer, I began doing the laundry.

You'd never write something that silly, you say? Well, try these, all taken from students' writings in a creative writing course.
- Standing on the balcony, the ocean view was magnificent.
- I heard that there was a revolution on the evening news.
- While taking out the trash, the sack broke.
- Having laid an egg weighing two pounds, the farmer proudly displayed his favorite ostrich before the photographers.

129

- Having given birth to six kittens, my girlfriend anxiously watched her exhausted cat, Whiskers.
- Ugly, warty creatures with protruding noses and bat-like wings, architecture students find gargoyles endlessly fascinating as expressions of the grotesque.
- The robber was described as a six foot-tall man with brown hair and blue eyes and a mustache weighing 150 pounds.

Please don't leave your readers laughing for the wrong reasons. Re-write the sentence.

∽ა⌒

One Letter Can Change Everything

When you are editing your manuscript, keep a sharp lookout for the following words. They differ by only one letter but have different uses and meanings.

ADVICE is a noun similar to recommendation.
ADVISE is a verb similar to recommend.
- I didn't ask for Samantha's advice, but she gave it to me anyway.
- The doctor advised me to drink more water when I exercise.

ALTAR is a raised structure in a church.
ALTER means to change.
- The congregation stood and faced the altar.
- The book is great; don't alter a word of it. (Hah! That's a sentence you'll almost never see.)

CAPITAL is a noun referring to a city or money, as well as an adjective that means main or that precedes the word punishment.
CAPITOL is a government building.
- Our capital goal is to raise the capital needed to fund the new project.
- Which architectural styles were popular when this capitol was built?

CAVALRY is a horse-mounted military unit.
CALVARY is a hill mentioned in the Bible.
- During the Civil War, cavalry units still ranked as elite troops.
- The Crucifixion took place at Calvary.

CITE is a verb meaning mention.
SITE is a noun referring to location (whether physical or on the Internet).
- Be sure you cite at least five sources in your next research paper.
- There are mixed opinions about the best site for the new residence hall.

COMPLEMENT is a noun or verb that refers to completeness. Note that "comple" begins both complement and complete.
COMPLIMENT is a noun or verb similar to praise.
- Bethany always wears a scarf to complement her outfit.
- Although his stage persona is extroverted, Boswell gets embarrassed every time someone compliments his acting abilities.

DESERT is a noun referring to a dry place or climate and a verb meaning leave.
DESSERT is a noun referring to a sweet food. The extra "s" in this word comes from the sweetness.
- I love water too much to live in a desert.
- Although Mary went to the party with Jon, she deserted him as soon as she found her other friends.
- My favorite dessert is warm chocolate cake with coconut ice cream.

FARTHER is the preferred word when describing physical distance.
FURTHER generally refers to figurative distance or distance in time.

- If I lived farther from campus, perhaps I would get more exercise.
- Housing is an important topic; let's discuss it further tomorrow.

ITS is the possessive form of the pronoun IT.
IT'S is a contraction of IT IS.
- The cow jumped over its fence.
- It's time to build a higher fence.

PRINCIPAL is an adjective meaning main or most important and a noun identifying a sum of money or the head of a school. Remember, "The principal of your school is your pal."
PRINCIPLE is a noun similar to rule or belief.
- The principal reason we hired Mr. Jones as the new principal is that he is extremely creative. [And I admit that sentence is too wordy!]
- Maxine adhered to three basic principles when she wrote her novels: revise, revise, revise.

STATIONARY means not moving.
STATIONERY is a noun referring to paper and other writing. Notice the "er" in both stationery and paper.
- Although the scenery was dull, Jim preferred the stationary bicycle in his basement.
- Sandra writes so many letters that she buys new stationery every month.

∽◦∾

A Few More Problematic Pairs

Here are some pairs (and one triplet) that are a bit more complicated than the previous list. Depending on where you live, some of them may sound identical, but they are different words.

ACCEPT is a verb that means agree with or receive.
EXCEPT is a preposition that means apart from.

- We accept all major credit cards.
- I accept your explanation of these differences
- Men are idiots . . . present company excepted.
- I like all vegetables except turnips.

ACUTE means sharp, as in an angle. It also describes a disease that rapidly develops and gets worse.
CHRONIC illness or problem may also be severe, but it is long-lasting and lingering.
- She developed acute appendicitis.
- She has chronic hay fever.

ADVERSE means unfavorable or hostile.
AVERSE means having a strong feeling of repugnance or opposition.
- This summer we face adverse weather conditions.
- He is not averse to buying a lottery ticket now and then.

AFFECT is a verb that means to influence something.
EFFECT is a noun that means the result of something. (Just to complicate matters, these two words have specialized academic meanings, but for most of us, this distinction doesn't matter.)
Remember, if something affects you, it has an effect on you.
- The movie affected me so deeply that I cried all the way through it.
- Hot temperatures have an adverse effect on our ability to think clearly.

CONTIGUOUS means touching or adjoining in space.
CONTINUAL means repeated frequently.
CONTINUOUS means uninterrupted in time or space.
- Alaska is not one of the forty-eight contiguous states because it does not share a border with any other state.
- His continual disruptions disturb those who attend our meetings.
- The continuous murmur of the stream outside my window puts me to sleep.

DISCREET means circumspect or careful about what we say.
DISCRETE means having separate and distinct parts.
- Congressmen are expected to be discreet about information they learn as part of their duties.
- Our three branches of government should remain discrete. (As well as discreet, of course.)

DISINTERESTED means not having a bias or personal stake in an issue.
UNINTERESTED means to have no interest in something.
- A disinterested person should settle the argument.
- I am uninterested in celebrity gossip.

EMIGRATION is leaving a country.
IMMIGRATION is arriving into a new country. It all depends on where you stand in relation to the act.
- His parents were hurt by his emigration from the old country.
- The newly settled west welcomed his immigration because he brought much need skills with him.

FLOUT means to ignore a rule openly and defiantly.
FLAUNT means to show off.
- He flouts traffic signs by speeding right through them.
- He enjoys flaunting his fancy new car.

PAST, the adjective, refers to something that has previously occurred.
PASSED, the verb, is the past tense of pass.
- Please forget about my past failures.
- This time I passed my driver's test.

∽꘍∾

More Ways to Improve Your Diction
Look for words that are redundant or indefinite.

- BACK - He turned back... Better: He turned...
- UP (when the direction is obvious) - He jumped up onto the porch. Better: He jumped onto the porch.
- DOWN (when the direction is obvious) - He looked down at his feet. Better: He looked at his feet. Don't fly over, across, up, down, north, south, east, or west to Atlanta. Simply fly to Atlanta. You usually can't tell which direction you're going in an airplane, anyhow.

Reconsider your use of IT, THEY, SOME, MANY, FEW Name the object. Who are they? Quantify some, many and few.

If you mention an animal, don't refer to the creature as a cat, dog, horse, etc. Give the specific breed, sex, or color. If you mention a car, give the make, model, or color. If you mention time, define the duration—ten minutes or thirty days.

Check for those words that occur frequently throughout the manuscript and substitute another similar word.

- WALKED – try strode, ambled, sauntered, strolled, shuffled, staggered.
- RAN – try jogged, scurried, scampered, hurried, dashed, rushed, loped.
- CRIED—whimpered, sobbed, sniveled, bawled, wailed, blubbered, howled.

Consider your adjectives. Are they bland? Why? Choose adjectives that will and play on the senses and add sparkle to the text.

- COLD – How cold? Icy, bone-chilling, numbing, frosty, artic.
- HOT – How hot? Blistering, broiling, sizzling, scalding.

❧

Five Words

Most of us recognize good writing when we see it, but we don't often interrupt our sheer delight in a passage to analyze it. We don't ask what it was that made that particular group of words stand out. We simply move on, anxious to read more of "the good stuff." The same sort of thing happens with bad writing, although our responses are more varied. Sometimes we nod off over a book or article because it is not interesting enough to keep our minds alert. Other times, we put the book down and forget we were trying to read it. When the writing is really bad, teachers shake their heads in despair, and slap a C- on the paper. And once again, we move on in search of something better, without taking the time to figure out exactly what it was that elicited our sighs.

The process of writing is complicated—and so different for each writer—that I was struggling with how to describe the difference between good and bad writing. One morning, help arrived in the shape of an e-mail from a colleague who was deep into grading at the moment. She simply passed along a paragraph that summed up the distinction:

This sentence has five words. Here are five more words. Five-word sentences are fine. But several together become monotonous. Listen to what is happening. The writing is getting boring. The sound of it drones. It's like a stuck record. The ear demands some variety. Now listen. I vary the sentence length, and I create music. Music. The writing sings. It has a pleasant rhythm, a lilt, a harmony. I use short sentences. And I use sentences of medium length. And sometimes, when I am certain the reader is rested, I will engage him with a sentence of considerable length, a sentence that burns with energy and builds with all the impetus of a crescendo, the roll of the drums, the crash of the cymbals—sounds that say listen to this, it is important.

This is one of those ideas that I want to write on a rock: "The ear demands variety."

14. Hire an Editor

I asked a Facebook friend who happens to run a book design business to give me an example of what a professional editor can do for your book. Here's the example she offered.

Our editor once found a mistake in a cookbook—a collection of easy supper recipes using pre-cooked rotisserie chickens from the grocery store. At the front of the book, the author provided a warning that these recipes were to be made only with cooked chicken, never with uncooked chicken. All well and good. But our editor noticed that within each recipe itself, the list of ingredients simply said "chicken." Of course, the author knew what she meant, but in real life, people flip through a cookbook and don't always re-read the first pages. This one little correction, changing "chicken" to "cooked chicken," probably prevented a lot of bellyaches (or worse).

❧

Choosing an Editor

The process of giving birth to a novel seems to go on indefinitely. Let's start with the problem of choosing an editor. I heard what all of you had to say about the need for an editor. I heard you say that I would be my worst critic, although that's not really true. I'm more critical of my own work than I am of others. And my forty-four years experience in teaching, correcting, and nitpicking other folks' writing ought to count for something.

Still, I heard you and set out to hire an editor. It was a frustrating experience.

One publisher offered to provide an editor for me, one who would produce exactly the manuscript the publisher wanted. (Note: no question of what I wanted.) Cost: $3200 to $3400 depending on the length of the book. Uh . . . no.

Editor number two set a flat fee of $2400, without even knowing how long the manuscript was. His qualifications included six months of experience and a shiny new masters degree in English. I don't think so!

Editor number three read and edited a selection from the manuscript for free (bonus points), but found no spelling errors, no grammatical errors, no outright punctuation errors, and no problems with dialog, transitions, or diction. How flattering, but . . . really? The next time through it, I found several. This one wanted $2800, more or less, based on exact word count, and left me wondering what I would be paying for besides an ego boost.

Each time I rejected one of these, I did another read-through and polished the manuscript myself. It was starting to look pretty good, but—still hearing all your warnings—I knew I needed some fresh eyes. Some of you may remember my solution. I sent out a call for volunteer readers—people who would be willing to read the book in manuscript form and comment. I ended up with a panel of readers. They included someone who knows the South Carolina setting well, a Civil War re-enactor to catch the military flubs, an engineer with an eye for detail, a wife and mother who was looking for a "good read" at the end of the day, and a fellow writer who is aware of the many pitfalls we all slip into.

They have been enormously helpful, and the book is better because of their efforts.

∽◦∾

It's the Little Things that Get You!

Even if you decide to hire a professional editor, you'll need to do a fair amount of polishing before you send your book off.

Believe me, every criticism is going to sting, no matter how well intentioned or accurate it is. Save yourself some grief by doing some preliminary editing.

"One of the best things you can do to improve your writing is to just read through all of it and get rid of all the little words that you really don't need."

Now there's a fine, wordy sentence for you. What does it say? How about:

"Improve your writing by removing unnecessary words."

Yes, you're right. That's going to reduce your word count, which is why I don't worry too much about wordiness while I'm doing NaNoWriMo exercises. But while reducing your word count, it's also reducing your reader's irritation, and that's a good thing.

Here's a list of little words you don't need. Try reading each sentence without that extra word. Don't they all sound better?

- SO (as in "I was so glad to see him.") There's an exception here: "so" is acceptable only when it is followed by a "that"—as in "She was SO short THAT she only saw people from the waist down."
- VERY (as in "I was very, very tired.")
- THAT (as in ("I thought that I should leave.")
- ALTHOUGH ("Although, I'm not sure I should.""")
- JUST ("I was just beginning to get sleepy.")
- YET ("She hasn't arrived yet.")
- RATHER ("It seemed rather rude.")
- EVEN ("Even the other guests were bored.")
- SORT OF ("The milk was sort of soured.")
- IN SPITE OF ("I was irritated in spite of myself.")
- PERHAPS ("I could, perhaps, take a nap.")
- QUITE ("I was quite tempted to do it.")
- FOR A MOMENT ("I hesitated for a moment.")
- THEN ("Then I walked out.")
- SUDDENLY ("Suddenly I stopped.")
- ALMOST ("The roast beef was almost burned.")

I copied the list from another blogger several years ago, and I've used it ever since. Once your manuscript is complete, go to the "find and replace" function in your word processor, and scan the whole manuscript for each word. That means you'll go through the whole manuscript about eighteen times, but you'll be surprised at how many other errors you'll spot along the way.

Every time you find one of the words on the list, ask yourself if the meaning of the sentence changes when you take the word out. If it doesn't, drop it. Now granted, the sentences above sound a bit choppy once the "little words" are gone, but you can always add a more inventive phrase when you need to.

One final caveat: Don't do a blind "find and remove." You have to look at each instance and make a conscious decision. The word "that," for example, is necessary in many places. (This one is spoiled; THAT one is not.)

And sometimes these words make an important point about your character. If she always states her opinion by prefacing it with "perhaps," we realize she is unsure of herself. In her conversation, leave it in. In your narrative, take it out.

ဢၭ

Are You Ever Finished Editing?

We've talked about awkward wording, misused words, bland adjectives, misplaced commas, and boring verbs. What else could possibly be wrong? Before you decide your book is perfect, let's try one final round of tweaking.

Eliminate all instances of passive voice. A sentence will usually be much stronger if the subject is the one doing the action, not the object of someone else's action. "I was spanked by my father" is whiny. "My father spanked me" is angry and accusatory.

How do you find passives? The various forms of the verb "to be" (am, is, are, was, were, being, been) do not necessarily make a sentence passive, but it is hard to imagine a passive sentence without one. Every time you find one of these words, ask yourself if the subject is acting or being acted upon. If the subject is not the actor, re-write the sentence.

- "The child was being beaten by a bully." (Passive—the subject is having something done to him.)
- "The child was beating the drum." (Active—the subject did the action.)

Check your dialogue. Does it sound like real people talking? Try eavesdropping on real conversations while riding a bus or waiting in a checkout line. You'll see that people don't often use complete sentences, and speakers don't politely wait their turn. They jump in whenever they feel like it.

Have you used too much description in identifying the speakers? Is it really necessary to identify the speaker? If your characters are strong, they will have distinctive speech patterns that will automatically identify them. You can usually get rid of "Tom said," before every pronouncement. The only exception to that rule may be when you are handling a conversation in which more than three people are involved. And even in that circumstance, you probably don't want to use any tags beyond "said" or "asked" or "answered."

Consider this example: "I don't want to leave," she sniffled. Now, she may have said that, and she may have been sniffling at about the same time, but she can't sniffle (which involves breathing in) and speak (which involves breathing out) at the same time. If you are determined to keep every word, then punctuate it as two sentences: "I don't want to leave." She sniffled.

Don't be too descriptive. Let the speaker's words tell the reader how the words were said. Consider this horrible example: "Help!" she shouted helplessly. It conveys the same information four times in four words: the word itself; the exclamation point; the descriptive tag, 'she shouted": and that ridiculous adverb at the end. "Help!" tells the reader everything necessary.

Vary your sentence structure and length. Don't start every sentence by giving subject—verb—object. But don't start every sentence with a conjunction, either. Personally, I really have to watch my habit of starting with an adverb or prepositional phrase. All grammatical sentences are acceptable, but you need variety to keep your reader awake.

Keep each page visually attractive. Try staring at the page from across the room. Do you have enough white space to make the page look interesting? Make sure you don't have lengthy segments of narrative. Dialog helps to keep up the pacing. Perhaps you give more description than is needed. Does the page look like a solid block of print? Perhaps you need to break it into several shorter paragraphs, or add some dialogue in the middle.

At the other extreme, you don't want a whole page full of dialog in which each person speaks only one or two words. If the page has a narrow band of print at the left margin, and gaping areas of white space on the right, you'll need to break up the conversation with paragraphs of description.

Be sure your facts are consistent from one section of the book to another. If a character has blue eyes in Chapter One, they probably won't turn brown in Chapter Four. If you speak of summer heat, don't send your characters out sledding in the next few days. Check dates extra carefully. Don't let a character die and then come back to life, unless you are into zombies and vampires.

Check your transitions. Chapters should wrap up some loose ends but leave enough questions unanswered to make your reader want to keep reading. A new chapter may switch point of view, or location, or jump from one period of time to another. But if such changes take place, be sure to make them clear at the start. The first words of a new chapter may need to be some variety of these:

- Meanwhile, back at the police station . . .
- The next day, Tom traveled to . . .
- After school, the children . . .
- When the plane landed in Paris, . . .

Editing your work using these questions will produce a more readable book. Will it then be perfect? Of course not. You still must be on the alert for omitted articles and prepositions. Look for spots where you may have done some cutting and pasting, leaving a few extraneous words behind. Other proofreading tricks may help. Some people swear by reading the book backwards, which may draw your attention to misspelled words. Enlist the help of willing friends, who may spot details your own eyes keep overlooking.

And then, once you've exhausted your own editing ability, pay for a professional editor.

∽❀∾

Editing Your Kindle Edition

I don't think it is possible to say this too often: Electronic books are not print books. They need a whole different approach to editing. Once your paper version has been edited and the copy arranged attractively on the page, you can step back and admire it. Both edges are justified. The lines are well spaced. No obvious gaps appear in your words. If you've had a specialist do your layout, you can feel confident that there are no rivers of white space running through your page to distract the reader. And best of all, that page layout will never change into a form you do not like.

None of that is true of an electronic book, simply because the nature of an e-text is to be fluid. Many people like their Kindles because of their ability to increase or decrease the font size to suit their own visual needs. I've touted that myself. But you understand what that means, right? Increase the font by two points and words are no longer the same length.

A hyphenated word may look fine in print, but come off badly in an e-book, because the hyphen may now appear in the middle of a line. One early reviewer of *Beyond All Price* criticized the book severely because she thought I had been trying to make fun of a speech defect by putting in random hyphens. Her reaction may have been wrong-headed, but it warned me of the problems that can result from failing to examine an electronic version carefully enough.

Another source of trouble lies with hidden codes, such as spacing between words. Even if you turn on a program that lets you see the coding, the tiny dot that indicates a single space can be almost invisible. I strongly recommend that before you convert your text to any electronic format—and before you let someone else do the coding for you—you use the search and replace function of your word processor to comb your document over and over again. Here are some of the things you need to look for.

First, remove all automatic hyphenation. Only the person doing the final layout can determine when and if a word needs to be hyphenated. Leave the right justification to an expert.

Next, look for hyphens used in place of a dash. We all use hyphens this way, I suspect. There's no dash key except in special symbols charts, so we substitute a double hyphen. Sometimes, our word processors automatically change a double hyphen to an em dash. But if yours doesn't, you will have to search for two hyphens and then do an automatic replace with the correct dash.

You'll also need to note that when two hyphens separate numbers, they need to be replaced with an en dash, which is slightly shorter. But you're still not done. You also need to search for dashes with spaces on either side and remove those spaces. I know. I know! I like the appearance of the space myself, but it will not translate correctly to an electronic version. Trust me on this.

Remove all tab stops, even those that you've been trained to use to indent the first word of a new paragraph. Indenting the first word of a paragraph can cause horrible alignment problems on a Kindle. And don't substitute five spaces for a tab stop. That will only make the situation worse. If you must indent your paragraphs, set the indent under "Paragraph formatting."

While we're talking about spaces, do a search and replace for two spaces in a row, and automatically replace them with one space. My old typing teacher insisted on two spaces at the end of a sentence, but that is no longer the rule. You may know that, but your right thumb, which adds the spaces, will betray you if you are a good touch typist.

Search for abbreviations and put them in small caps: 6 AM not 6 A. M. or 6 a.m. You may find the small cap function under format and then font.

Forget what your English teacher told you and put all punctuation marks inside quotation marks: ?" not "?

And speaking of quotation marks, change all straight quotes to curly quotes. Then be prepared for more trouble. If you have had to use a single quotation mark to create an apostrophe at the beginning of a word to indicate pronunciation, it will probably be curved the wrong way.

Consider this sentence: *Y'all don't come from 'round here, do ya'?* Look at *y'all* and *don't* and then compare it with *'round*. To turn that curly mark around, you will have to type it like this: *a'round*. Then remove the *a* and you get *'round*. For your sake, I hope you never even have the problem, but for me it's a constant annoyance as I try to duplicate slave speech.

Check your numbers to make sure you've used the numerals 1 and 0, not the letters l and O.

Finally, check your hard returns (paragraph markers) to make sure you have not used more than one to create vertical spacing.

The process of cleaning up these tiny errors can be tedious and time consuming, but it is a detail that marks the difference between an amateur and a professional. If you want your book to translate to an electronic version and still look good, take all the time this process requires.

15. Reject the Get-Rich-Quick Schemes

It sometimes seems that for every aspiring author, there is a shady book publisher waiting to take those dreams and turn them into cash for their own pockets. In order to succeed as a self-published author, you must constantly be alert for scam artists and their overblown promises of instant fame and wealth. You need to understand how book publishers can fleece you and how different types of presses work.

℞℞℞

Choosing Your Printing Company

Vanity presses have been around a long time. They will publish almost anything short of pure pornography, if the author agrees to pay all expenses. The author keeps all rights to the book and retains all profits, but these deals come with the requirement that the author purchase a large number of books up front. Unless you have a huge empty room you can fill with unwanted books, steer clear of any deal that says, "We'll publish your book if you buy 3,000 copies, or 30,000 copies at whatever price we want to charge you." The press gets the money for the books up front; you must recoup all the expenses by selling the books yourself. How many friends do you have?

Subsidy presses may sound like a better deal. They still charge the author for most expenses, although they may offer a few limited services such as marketing or editing. They retain all the rights to the books, and you get to sell them by sending people to the company to make their purchase. The company makes a huge profit and the author gets a small royalty, sometimes as little as 5% to 10% of the proceeds. On average, they sell about forty copies per title.

Print-On-Demand sounds even better. Thanks to the miracles of digital printing, books are only printed when they are sold. No one gets stuck with a huge unmovable inventory. However, most of these companies still charge large fees up front by offering package deals of services. You must pay them to do your cover, your layout, your editing, your press releases, and your marketing, and you get only a part of the proceeds of the sales. Most also insist on providing the ISBN, which gives them the rights to your book. Care to sell your soul while you're at it?

Self-publishing print-on-demand, however, turns out to be an easy category because there are so few legitimate choices. After I've looked at all the deals and one-time great offers, I can recommend only two companies—CreateSpace, which is the POD arm of Amazon, and Lightning Source, which is a branch of Ingram, the retail book distribution giant. In both cases, you can purchase services that you need, but you are not required to pay for anything you prefer to do for yourself. With CreateSpace, it is theoretically possible to have your books printed and distributed on Amazon.com at no charge. They make books available to you on a copy-by-copy basis for a small fee that covers the printing cost, and you can sell them for whatever the traffic will bear. You retain all rights.

Notice that I said "theoretically." In the real world, you are going to need some services. I chose to have CreateSpace do my layout and my cover, based on my own rough design. I did my own editing because I had extensive editing experience. I also continue to pay CreateSpace a small percentage of the profits from each book they sell on Amazon.com, but that seems only fair, since they are paying for advertising, handling, and shipping.

I made one additional purchase, which I came to regret. I paid CreateSpace to do my press releases. The releases were sloppily done and showed little understanding of the book. I had to demand that they be redone several times before I was satisfied. The company then sent those releases out to a list of some 10,000 outlets—TV stations, radio programs, newspapers, magazines, talk shows, and libraries. But out of the entire list of recipients, I received exactly one inquiry for further information. And it came from my own local newspaper. Lesson learned the hard way.

How do you choose? Every author has an opinion. For me, CreateSpace (except for their press releases) was totally satisfactory. They were responsive when I had questions, and they turned out a superior product. People who use Lightning Source are also satisfied, although Lightning Source offers fewer services and expects its authors to do more of the work. It's a toss-up, depending upon how computer savvy you are.

Once you've made your choice, save your manuscript as a PDF file, open an account with the company, and upload the files. Voila! Once I approved the page layout and cover design, I had my books in six days!

◦◦◦◦

Contracting for Other Services

Let's start with the book cover. By all means, start to think about your cover early. Readers are confronted with millions of choices when they look for a book, and your cover needs to be able to catch their attention quickly.

Try walking into a bookstore with no real purpose in mind. Just stroll around and notice which books catch your eye. Which ones fairly jump off the display table to say, "Hey!" and which ones make you curious once you have taken a closer look? Many factors go into book cover design, and unless you already have artistic ability or design experience, you may not immediately understand why some covers are better than others. Look at how many different elements appear in your favorite covers. Is there one image or many? Are the colors a hint about the content? Does the cover image wrap around the book from front to back? Do you like cutouts? embossing? glitter?

When you've found a few designs you like, try walking away from them and looking back at a distance. While seeing your book prominently displayed on a bookstore table is the ideal, how will prospective readers actually encounter it? Will it stand out from others of the same type? Will nothing but the spine show on a shelf? Will buyers go online and see only a thumbnail version? And if so, are the elements on the cover big enough to be visible in a thumbnail? All of these are issues you should understand before the actual design process begins.

But design it at this stage? Not so fast! Are you experienced enough to do your own design? I know I wasn't. I had an idea of what I wanted to show on the cover, but it took a professional to do the actual positioning, the trim sizing, and the font selection. Depending on what company you choose to handle the production of your books, you may need to pay for their design services or hire a designer to prepare to cover copy for you. Don't scrimp here. A poorly designed cover can lose a prospective sale in a few seconds. At least wait until you have production details set before you make a final decision on the cover.

∽◡∾

The Challenge of Book Layouts

Sometimes I suspect that today's great strides in technology have given us too much confidence in our ability to "do everything." My case in point? The current tendency for authors to assume they can produce a great-looking book by using nothing more than Microsoft Word and then saving it in PDF format. You've seen the results, I'm sure—the book that fairly shouts "Amateur printer!" at you as you pick it up. Here are some of the things that can go wrong when an author tries to do his own page layouts.

Text is hard to read. Even if you avoid those cutesy fonts that are designed to look like they are written in chalk by a third-grader, it is all too easy to choose the wrong font for the right purpose. Fonts like Garamond or Baskerville are designed with serifs—those little feet or flourishes at the ends of the letters. They are not there for decoration; they are designed to carry the eye from one letter to the next. When you're writing large blocks of text, they make reading much easier. Sans serif fonts, such as Ariel or Helvetica, are better suited to headings and chapter titles, where you want the individual word to stand out.

Pages look too crowded or show too much white space. Every font has slightly different spacing. For example, Garamond will require 30% more pages than Times New Roman to display the same document. Decisions about which to use depend on many factors, such as your intended audience, the number of internal breaks in the pages, the lengths of paragraphs, or predetermined page limitations.

Typesetting is flawed. The errors that can happen are almost too many to name. Margins change in width from page to page. Paragraphs are separated by an extra line but also indented. (It is correct to do either one, but never both.) Words that should be in italics are underlined instead. (The underlining is a printer's cue to set the type in italics. Underlining should never appear in the finished text.) Straight quotes, like those from an old-fashioned typewriter are used instead of the curly ones that all publications now use. The right-hand margin is not justified. Some lines are really short rather than hyphenated. Worse, the right-hand margins are justified, but some words have huge gaps between letters to stretch them to reach the left margin.

Page numbering is off. Books follow a number of conventions that you may ignore to your own peril. For example, the right-hand pages have odd numbers, and left-hand pages have even numbers. Cross them up and you will confuse even readers who do not notice the actual numbering. Also, new chapters always start on a right-hand page. That means that if one chapter ends on a right-hand page, the next page is left blank. If you have chapter headings on each page, they should not appear on a blank page or on the starting page of a new chapter.

A book should not look like a blog, even if, like this one, it originally was a blog. Don't use bold type to stress words. Forget about using boxes around some of the text. And avoid clipart or lots of stock photos.

If you learn those rules, will you be able to produce your own book layout? That's still doubtful. My suggestions here will work for someone who only wants to turn out a small quantity of books, with limited distribution. I tried this myself, with a cookbook I put together for the Lions Clubs of western Tennessee. Originally I printed only 100 copies, sold them all to fellow Lions (mostly people who had a recipe in the book!), and raised $1000.00 for one of our local charities. Later I revised it a bit and sold another 150 or so to Lions from out of state when they attended a conference in Memphis.

When I look at the book now, I am fairly pleased with its typography, although the font is childish. Page numbering is correct, margins are justified, paragraph spacing is correct, and I managed to fill any white spaces with lots of cute little clipart (which now makes me shudder.) The book served its purpose, but no one looking at it would mistake it for a professionally designed or published book.

I might recommend the Microsoft Word or Apple Pages book layout programs if you plan to produce a book of anecdotes for your class reunion, if you're helping your ten-year-old niece to "publish" her first short story, or if you simply want to preserve some family stories for future generations. If, however, you have written a wonderful book whose content can compete with professionally produced books in its genre, don't spoil its first impression with amateurish layout. Hire a professional.

16. Market, Market, Market

Authors are frequently surprised to find that book printers and publishers expect them to handle all their own publicity, advertising, and marketing. Yes, that used to be the job of the publisher. But you wanted to self-publish, remember? Once your book comes off the press, your work really begins.

⟲⟳

Your Elevator Speech

It's flattering when someone expresses an interest in your book, and you'll be tempted to launch into a full description. If the person is kind, he may hear a bit, but most people today—your agent, a reader, the publisher, bookseller or organization you want to speak for—all want concise reasons why they would be interested in your book. They are really thinking, "So what? Why would I want to buy your book?" You don't want to bore your prospective readers or turn them off with too much detail. What they want is a quick summary of your book—your 30-60 second elevator speech.

Why is it called an "elevator speech?" Imagine that the encounter takes place on a moving elevator. You have only the time before the door opens to make your sale. Without a 30-second description that states the book title, the intended audience, the main benefit to the reader, and what makes it unique, you lose the opportunity to give someone a reason to buy. You can also use this one to two-sentence blurb at any business meeting or appointment where you only have a few seconds to impress.

What you include in your speech will depend on the book itself and on the nature of the audience. If the book is non-fiction, it will be easy to state the contents—"a history of. . . " or "how to . . ." If you're pitching the book to a publisher, you'll want to emphasize the audience for which it is written. If you already know something about your listener, you can tailor the benefits to meet his needs. At a convention of novelists, for example, you could quickly describe the conflict and crisis.

You'll end up creating several elevator speeches before you find one that works in most situations. When you're satisfied, practice it until it comes automatically. Here are a couple of examples of where to start.

For a non-fiction title or a book like my own *Beyond All Price*, I usually concentrate on subject matter.

State the title. You want the listener to remember it once he steps off the elevator. *"Beyond All Price"* . . . ."

Describe the intended audience, making sure it will appeal to the listener. *"Beyond All Price" gives people interested in the Civil War—whether professional historian or history buff—a clearer understanding of what life was like for an army nurse during that tumultuous period.*

Add a few major benefits if the elevator is still moving. *"Beyond All Price" gives people interested in the Civil War—whether professional historian or history buff—a clearer understanding of what life was like for an army nurse during that tumultuous period. Nellie Chase's experiences expose her to the limitations of medical knowledge, the on-going problem of what to do with slaves once they were freed, and the restraints placed on a woman by nineteenth-century social customs."* You can say all of that in thirty seconds or less.

If your book is a novel, you may want to emphasize plot and character rather than benefits. Here's another outline:

Describe the lead character. *Nellie Chase is an abused wife. . . .*

Set the situation. *Nellie Chase is an abused wife who signs on as a nurse with a Union Army regiment during the Civil War.*

Establish her goal. *Nellie Chase is an abused wife who signs on as a nurse with a Union Army regiment during the Civil War. She is hoping for a new start, one that will allow her to atone for past mistakes and give her life a purpose.*

Describe the villain that stands in her way. *Nellie Chase is an abused wife who signs on as a nurse with a Union Army regiment during the Civil War. She is hoping for a new start, one that will allow her to atone for past mistakes. A narrow-minded chaplain tries to drive her out of the regiment by questioning her morality and forces her to find her life's purpose in an even more challenging role.*

Whichever approach you decide to use, you will be prepared for that quick moment when a sale or a contract depends on what you say in the next thirty seconds.

⁊◌⁊

A Virtual Launch Party

I held a virtual launch party for the release of my new Civil War novel, *Beyond All Price*. Like most self-published and print-on-demand authors, I had complete responsibility for promoting and marketing the book. If I didn't call attention to it, no one else was going to. I also happen to be a firm believer in the future of the e-book, so it seemed particularly appropriate to have an e-party. It was also cheaper, of course, and a bit less self-congratulatory, to use the Internet for the book's introduction, rather than holding a small party for the folks I knew. Here's how I went about it.

My publishing imprint is Katzenhaus Books. The company website was already up and running at Vistaprint. I wanted the launch to be connected to that site somehow, but at the same time separate and special. The answer was a second site, opened for a four-month period. Its content could be linked to the company website when needed. I started planning the party in July 2010, as soon as I had finished approving the final proofs for both the paperback and the Kindle editions. The party itself was set for September 15-17.

The party website had many pages, starting with a welcome page that set a festive tone with balloons and confetti. The book itself had its own page, with pictures of the cover, the cover blurb, an excerpt, and links to the company website, including the ordering information. Next came a fun page—what's a party without a few games? There were some bad jokes, a mystery puzzle, and a cartoon cat video, among other oddities.

Refreshments were easy. Visitors found a revolving buffet table with pictures of the food on offer and the recipes if they were really hungry. All the items on the buffet were dishes from the novel. Door prizes and give-aways had their own page, which also included an opt-in box, from which I could begin to create a dedicated e-mail list.

The real key to the success of the party, however, came from my invited guests—seven authors and seven Internet experts who wrote about writing. I interviewed the authors about their books and their similarities to my own work; the bloggers wrote articles about their own specialties—everything from creating a website, to the techniques of proofreading, punctuation, and the future of the publishing industry. Each one had a page that was featured for an eight-hour period during the launch. There the guests could post their own picture, pictures of their books, list their Internet addresses, and invite followers. All these materials remained accessible for the entire launch period and for a month afterward through a list of guest links.

I cannot begin to praise my guests enough. They not only took the time to write their articles; they also publicized the launch for me on their own blogs, websites, and social networks. When well-known authors tweeted, "I'll be appearing at this book launch at this time at this URL," their fans and readers followed them, and they learned about my book along the way. Their help was invaluable!

Questions remain, however. Was it successful? Would I do it again? What would I change? Well, for starters, I found out the party lasted too long. I thought I was cutting back from the only other online launch party I had seen—one that ran for an entire seven-day period. Mine started on Wednesday with a respectable number of visitors. The visits peaked around noon on Thursday, and limped through Friday, falling off to nearly nothing by Friday evening. I should have stopped Thursday night. The fun and games page was not particularly popular. People who took the time to visit the site wanted to know about my book or what my guests had to say. They didn't come to be entertained by other means. The opt-in box was badly placed. It should have been at the front of the site, not buried in the back. On the plus sign, people reacted well to most of my guests and enjoyed getting the recipes from the book. Who doesn't love food?

Sales were slow but steady through the first two days. I didn't sell as many copies as I would have liked, but those who ordered the book were new customers, most of whom I would not have met if it had not been for the launch party. And sales continued at the same pace for several weeks after the actual launch. I also gained new Twitter followers and Facebook friends. I'm glad I did it, and when my next book comes out, I'll probably do it again. Honestly? I had a blast!

A Virtual Book Tour

This method of reaching out to readers without having to do an actual book tour comes highly recommended. Personally, after doing one traditional book tour, I swore I'd never do another. My main objection to book tours? The author spends a great deal of time and money traveling from book store to library to coffee shop, never knowing whether the proprietor will have set up a successful get-together or not. Oh, I had some lovely experiences. One library put on a lavish spread of hors d'oeuvres and attracted a large and attentive audience. I sold a respectable number of books and felt like a celebrity.

But the next day, I found myself sitting in an empty bookstore—one whose owner had forgotten I was coming and had done no publicity at all. It was the day before a holiday weekend in a resort town full of visitors, and there was a good local tie to the book. But for three solid hours, not one soul entered the store. The single clerk and I made small talk as long as we could manage, and I ended up buying several books from her to make her feel better. I also absorbed the cost of a three-hour drive to get there and an overnight motel stay, along with meals. I felt like a failure, and the glow from the previous day's library visit faded when I looked at the negative balance in my account book.

A virtual book tour, on the other hand, is a wonderful device for building your following. Every time you post an interesting article on a new blog, you get a chance to add that person's followers to your own. Look for people with interests similar to your own, read their blogs until you are sure you like them (and their audiences), and then ask politely if you can do a guest post for them. If you offer their readers some information of value, you may create a long-term relationship that works for both of you. How do you do a virtual book tour? Here are the steps to follow.

Identify a time period of two or three weeks during which you can devote nearly all your time to making the tour work. You won't be traveling, but you'll be writing a new blog for every stop, doing promotional ads before each visit, and responding to comments and questions from many new readers. A friend recently finished a successful month-long tour and pronounced herself thoroughly exhausted. Don't start this campaign expecting it to be easy.

Identify bloggers who welcome guest appearances and whose readers are similar to your target audience. You probably can't sell historical fiction on a "Guns and Ammo" website. Look for blogs that have more readers than you do, but don't expect to find a welcome on a blog that already has thousands and thousands of followers. What you're hoping to do is establish a long-term relationship with other writers like yourself, bloggers with whom you can exchange appearances.

Contact each blogger with a personalized message that stresses what you have to offer. Send your book information, a good review, a press release, and your contact information. If you can, offer a free copy of your book. Specify the kinds of content you can provide—an interview, a blog on a specific topic, a contest in which you provide the prizes, or a book review. Be sure to check each site to see if it provides specific formats for such inquiries, and don't forget to include the dates of your tour.

Promote your appearances on Twitter, Networked Blogs, an event page on Facebook, or on your Author Central page on Amazon. Your host will appreciate the advance publicity, and you'll both gain additional readers.

Provide your host with your materials, including contact information, your professional photograph, and links to your sites well in advance of the date of your appearance. On the day of your appearance, check the site frequently and respond to all comments as quickly as possible. And finally, follow up with a thank you note and an offer to reciprocate.

∽ ℘ ℘

Press Release: Advertisement or Publicity?

You can pay to advertise your book, but you have to earn your good publicity. Please keep that distinction in mind when you create a new press release.

An advertising manager works in a newspaper office. His job requires him to fill the empty spaces between the columns and the articles with offers that readers will not be able to refuse. He will accept your ad for your new book happily, provided it is not obscene or offensive to the paper's paid subscribers. He may even help you come up with those key words designed to bring you sales: amazing, must-read, best-selling, award-winning, non-stop action, page-turner. For a "slightly higher" price you can add color, illustrations, quotes, testimonials, exclamation points, stars, banners, everything but the flashing lights and loudspeakers. The fancier your ad, the better he will like it. And the return? Well, there are no guarantees. All he can really offer is the chance to put your name and the title of the book in front of people, in the hope that they will pause on the page long enough to read what your ad says. After that, it is entirely up to your own words to entice the reader to buy what you have for sale.

A newspaper columnist also works in the office. Her job is to fill the spaces between the ads with interesting columns that will make readers stop, read, and remember what she has written. On those days when nothing burns down, no one murders a spouse, and the dog doesn't bite the mailman, the columnist will be on a desperate hunt for eye-catching news. No, she doesn't need a sales pitch, and she probably won't think it is important that you have a book for sale. She's looking for a human interest story, a tale of a struggling writer who finally wins an award, a librarian who makes a history-changing discovery, a visiting scholar with a story to tell, or an expert who has discovered the answer to someone's prayers. If you can couch your press release in those terms, the columnist will not only write your story but tell it in its most appealing format. And the return? Once again, your name and book title appear in the public eye. But now they are bathed in a much more favorable light. A column in a newspaper or magazine or an interview on the local radio station brings you favorable publicity, not advertising.

A good press release has great potential for attracting readers to your book, but it requires several contributions from you. It must be newsworthy. Its details must be clearly and concisely described. More important, it must be formatted correctly so that the columnist sees it as a professional presentation. Here are some suggestions on how to do that formatting. Everything should fit on a single page.

At the top of the page, put the words "FOR IMMEDIATE RELEASE" in all capital letters. That gives the journalist permission to use the information that follows.

- Skip a line and give the release date and the city of origin: "July 4, 1776, Philadelphia."

- Skip another line and write your headline. Keep it short and attention-grabbing. Type it on one line with the first letter of each word capitalized: "Patriots Declare Independence From England."
- Next comes a summary paragraph of about free to five lines, answering the standard questions " Who, what, where, when, and why."
- Further details appear in the body of the press release. This is the spot for plot summary, background information, and other relevant details. Keep this section to two or three paragraphs, each no longer than eight lines and separate the paragraphs with a blank line to make them easier to read. Be sure to write this section in third-person point of view. Imagine that you are the columnist, and see the information through her eyes.
- End with contact information: the name of the publishing company, their media contact person (who is probably you!), a phone number, mailing address, and an e-mail address. A fax number or website may also be useful. Make it as easy as possible for the reader to contact you or to get more information.
- Close with one of the printing symbols that lets readers know they have reached the end: --30-- or ###

Once you have your press release written, the final task is to get it into as many hands as possible, but make sure that they are the hands of people who will have a legitimate reason to care about your announcement. You'll find many offers from public relations people to handle your press releases. They promise to send them out to their standard lists of thousands of publications. Such services are not cheap, but they are all too often worthless.

Newspapers, libraries, radio and TV stations, alumni associations, and trade groups are all fair game for press releases, but only if you have some personal connection to them. If you live in Wyoming, a morning talk show on a Georgia TV station will probably not invite you as a guest. If you graduated from the University of Tennessee, the University of Florida does not want to hear of your accomplishments. On the other hand, your local high school or college newspaper may be looking for stories about alumni who have become famous. Your company headquarters may be proud to publicize an employee who has received an honor. Contact every news outlet within a short drive from your home, and make your availability clear.

Use your writing talent to gain that all-important publicity. It lasts much longer than an ad.

∽ა ია

The Value of Book Contests

Would you ever consider paying someone $100.00 for the privilege of entering a book contest? Sound like a scam? Well, think again. Book contests can help your marketing efforts in many ways. Granted, $100.00 sounds like a lot of money to someone who is only selling a few books a month, and that amount does not include the cost of the book itself or your mailing costs, either. But a charge of $100.00 or less is usually a legitimate one. Running a book contest is an expensive proposition. After all, someone has to pay for medals, winner's stickers, websites, postage, ads, and all the other related expenses. By charging relatively small fees, the sponsors of these contests are making it possible to reward many more fledgling authors.

Are you afraid the contest is rigged? If it has been operating for several years, you should be able to find a list of past winners. A legitimate contest should be listed in publications like *Writers Markets* or on the websites of the sponsoring organizations. By all means, do your homework, and find a contest that appears reputable and designed for writers like you. Then read the rules and jump in.

Are you afraid of rejection? Failure is something you might as well get used to if you've decided to become a writer. Every one of us could paper a room with our rejection letters. Lots of books don't make it. I saw a statistic recently that indicated that out of 1.2 million books published in the past year, only about 3000 of them ever sell more than 50,000 copies. Welcome to the 99.75% of us who should not quit our day jobs. We all flounder together. A book contest may be what you need to overcome that fear of failure. Even if you don't win a thing, you'll benefit.

You may be surprised to find that the act of entering a contest makes you feel more confident about your own abilities. After all, you have written a book that meets the qualifications of an organization that awards good writing. You've followed guidelines and met a deadline. Best of all, you've proved to yourself that you have faith in your own work. That's important.

If you don't win, be sure to follow up. Many such contests are willing to provide you with their reviewers' comments, so that you can learn what it was that they did not like about your book. If you can learn from your first attempt, you'll have a better shot at future contests. Also take a look at the winners. Read their books or at least excerpts from them to get an idea of what the reviewers liked about them. That's another lesson learned.

And what if you do win? Even if you get nothing but an honorable mention sticker to put on your book, it will draw attention to your work and perhaps even help you sell more books. Publishers, agents, booksellers, and buyers are all impressed by those shiny little seals. A gold seal makes you stand out from that whole crowd of 1.2 million book authors. Win one award, at any level, and you can call yourself an award-winning author. Put that on your website, display the seal or your medal everywhere you can, and use the award as a major factor in your marketing efforts.

This past year, I entered two contests—the Pinnacle Book Achievement Awards and the annual Military Writers Society of America Book Awards. Neither contest offered a Pulitzer or a Man Booker prize, but I profited greatly from both. Both contests give awards in many genres and are open to both traditional publishers and self-publishers. Both publish reviews of their book entries, and any self-publisher can use another book review. Remember that getting favorable publicity is a major part of your marketing effort.

Pinnacle Awards, presented by the North American Booksellers Exchange (NABE), come out every three months, but the award seal does not give dates. I won my "Best Historical Fiction" award for Summer 2011, but the seal shows only the award, not the date. The Military Writers Society of America (MWSA) awarded the same book a bronze medal for Biography. Again, the resulting seal shows only the award, not the date or genre.

As soon as these contests announced their winners, my book sales began to improve. The NABE award resulted in my book being given a prominent display at two major book trade shows on the west coast. To receive my medal from MWSA, I traveled to their convention, where I met wonderfully congenial and supportive writers. I am much the richer for the experiences these contests have given me. They were well worth the entry fees.

17. Embrace New Technology

Do you really need to publish your book as an eBook? Won't that hurt your "real" book sales? Isn't there something perverse about writing a book and then publishing it as something that is not really a book? Over on one of the discussion lists I follow, there's a debate going on right now about publishing in both hardback and paperback editions at the same time. That's dangerous enough. Why complicate matters by putting your hard work out there in some electronic form that people can't even pick up? I've heard all these questions, and I understand the unwillingness to jump into a new-fangled technology. But please pay attention. You need to do this!

☙❧

Why You Must Publish an eBook

I understand how satisfying it is to pick up a beautiful book and be able to say, "Hey! I wrote this. This is mine." The thrill of finding your book in a bookstore—maybe on a table at the front of the store—is worth all the effort you put into it. But what do you really want? You write because you want others to read. If you want to keep your words secret, get a diary and hide it under your mattress. If you want living, breathing readers who will engage in your ideas, you have to go out and find them where they are. And the truth is that more and more readers are turning to e-books as their reading choice.

I'm not going to go into all the reasons why people like e-books. Let's accept the fact that readers are turning more and more often to their electronic gadgets instead of lugging around a book. And when they are looking for a good read, they have lots of choices. According to one set of figures I saw recently, there are more than 900,000 books currently for sale in the Kindle Store. With an e-reader, you can also have access to an additional 1.8 million out-of-copyright books published prior to 1923. And they are free. With all those choices, who, except your mother, would pay $25.00 for your real book?

The question is not whether to publish an e-book, but in what format. Should you go with Kindle, or Apple's iBook, or the Nook, or the Sony reader? The answer is yes. Until the industry settles down and creates a single standard, you need to put your material out there in every available format. That sounds daunting. If you're a complete technological klutz, you can hire someone to do the formatting for you, but it's really not all that tough.

Start with Kindle. Kindle editions appear as format choices on Amazon.com, right along with your print edition, and a large share of the reading audience will find your e-book there. Kindle offers complete instructions on how to submit your manuscript in acceptable format. They accept Word files (.doc) or .pdf, or .rtf among others. Follow their instructions, and your e-book will appeal like magic.

Then turn to Smashwords. These folks take your .doc file and convert your work into all the different formats needed for second-tier readers. They also handle the distribution of your files to the ordering websites of all of those different readers. There is no charge for that service, and they stand behind their work. Apple's iBook store recently tightened their standards for e-book coding and notified me that my version of *Beyond All Price* had coding errors. I simply forwarded the message to Smashwords, and they fixed the problem within hours. They make their money by featuring your book as a page in their own catalog and taking a small amount of the sales from that catalog as their profit. You get about 60% to 85% of the sale, without doing anything except letting them put your work out there.

On September 12, 2011, Smashwords founder Mark Coker, sent out the following e-mail message to all of their authors:

Smashwords reached another milestone yesterday. One of our authors published the three billionth word.

We reached two billion words four months ago, and one billion 11 months ago.

To put this in further context, in the last four months we averaged 8.3 million words a day. This works out to about 350,000 words per hour, 5,700 words per minute or almost 100 words per second. Can you hear the keyboards clicking?

Smashwords is an ebook publishing and distribution platform. We're simply a tool that enables the efficient publication, distribution and management of ebooks. Our mission is to unleash the literary talent of writers from every corner of the globe.

We're now publishing over 70,000 books from 28,000 authors. In our first year, 2008, we published 140 titles. That grew to 6,000 in 2009, 28,800 in 2010, and will likely surpass 90,000 this year.

There it is. No difficult formatting. No inventory to clutter your dining room. No sales pitches to deliver. No advertising to pay for. No sales to handle. No shipping to worry about. Just money coming in, steadily and reliably every month.

Why wouldn't you do this?

∽◦∾

Kindling a Controversy

I had a revealing conversation recently at a gathering of academics. One of them asked me how sales were going for *Beyond All Price*. I said they were slow but steady, and then commented that the Kindle version was selling particularly well. There was a moment of shocked silence. Now, I should have been prepared for that. I know these people pretty well, and I understand that they are all book lovers. I've been in their offices and seen the shelves weighted down with their personal libraries. Then the conversation went something like this:

"There's a Kindle edition? Are you happy about that?"

"Of course I am. I set it up."

"But . . . a Kindle? Do you actually have one?"

"I've had one for several years. I love it."

"But . . . it's not a real book."

"Of course it is. These days I don't read anything else."

"Oh." Skeptical looks, arched eyebrows, sighs, shrugs, and obvious dismissal followed.

Here's what we didn't say, because we really like each other and respect our collegiality:

THEM: "Oh, you poor old thing. This is what happens when you retire. You lose your academic standards and focus."

ME: "No, you're thinking like a Luddite! E-books are the wave of the future. I love old books, too, but there are untold advantages to electronic editions. You need to emerge from your book-lined cubbyhole now and then and see what's happening on the outside."

I don't want to go back over all the selling points for Kindle. You can find those all over the web. But here are some of the factors that particularly appeal to a retired old academic.

Ease of use. I've put in my years of carting loads of books everywhere I went. The Kindle fits in my purse and adds only ounces to its weight. When I'm reading a hefty volume, my arthritic thumbs no longer protest at the weight of the book itself, and the pages don't need a steady grip. I can hold the Kindle in one hand, or prop it on my knee.

Affordability. New books, even best sellers, are available for under $10.00, and some are ridiculously low-priced. Most of the time, my own *Beyond All Price* can be had for $2.99. I've also published two small e-books, one on Civil War cooking and the other on Civil War medical treatments. They're both downloadable at $ .99. *A Scratch with the Rebels*, the history of the Roundhead Regiment that sold at $24.95, is now only $9.95 in the Kindle Bookstore. And then there are the classics. Books that are out of copyright are not only readily available but usually free. You can download a whole set of Shakespearean drama or Agatha Christie mysteries without spending a dime. You don't even have to pay a shipping charge.

Space availability. When we moved into our new but downsized house, many wonderful books ended up in cartons in the garage or on a sale rack at the library. We simply did not have room for the collection that used to line my office walls. But my Kindle? It can hold 3,500 books, every one of them available instantly when I want a particular volume.

Convenience. No, I haven't lost my love of reading. I read more now than I ever did. On a beach? Sure. Sunlight, ocean breezes, and sand are no problem. On a plane? Of course. No plugs or cords needed, and no extra space in the carry-on bag. In a dentist's waiting room? A Kindle book is much better than a ragged magazine from 2005.

Transfer ability. The greatest benefit, for me, comes from the Kindle App. It is available free for tablet readers, smart phones, and desktop computers. I have a copy on every one of my electronic gadgets, and they all sync automatically. I can start reading on the Kindle, do a bit more on my iPhone in a boring meeting, read another chapter in my office while waiting for a computer program to update itself, and finish a suspenseful story on my lighted iPad in the middle of the night. Kindle keeps track of my place, no matter which device I'm using. No more dog-eared pages or bookmarks lost to devilish cats that love to pull them out of books.

My colleagues who shook their heads over my lack of academic purity might remember that I have long been an early-adapter. I love what's new if it makes life easier. As a medievalist, I revere those old twelfth-century volumes, handwritten by dedicated monks on the thinnest possible vellum. But I'd have been first in line when Gutenberg started cranking up his press. I was right there when the first Kindles became available.

⁓⁓⁓

Give Away $70,000 and Make a Profit

Kindle editions can be a goldmine, but it takes some doing. Price is key. There are thousands of people out there who only "buy" free books, and thousands more who won't buy anything until it ranks in the top 100 bestsellers. Here's one method to try if you're willing to take a risk.

There has been extensive research to show that if you price your book above $2.99, most customers simply won't buy it. So, you start by listing your book on Kindle at $2.99 (tops). Then go to Smashwords.com and get the book offered there as well. Publishing on Smashwords is free, and they will allow you to list your book as free. Do it, even though it hurts.

You have to get Smashwords involved, because Kindle doesn't let you make that final pricing decision to give the book away. Amazon decides when your book is offered for free, and when it comes off the free list and returns to the price you set. After a week or two of the free offer from Smashwords, the Kindle staff usually catches on that they are being undersold, and at that point they, too, will list your book as free. This is where it really starts to hurt. With any luck at all, you'll see your download figures jump.

Now, you won't be making any money, and the give-away usually lasts about a week. But in that "free period" you will have built name recognition and soared to a respectable place among the bestsellers. Kindle changes their best-seller rankings every hour, so you may reach the top and plummet to the bottom within hours. That doesn't matter. Once your book returns to the $2.99 level, the sales will continue, at least for a while—long enough for you to make some money.

I promise you it can work. It happened to me in August 2011. Here are my sales figures. In July, I was selling about one book a week (in a good week). Then my book went to "free" and in seven days, there were 35,560 copies downloaded. Yes, if all those people had bought their copies for $2.99, I would have been $70,000 richer. But then, the people who ordered it for free were not likely to pay for it. These were not lost sales; they were new readers.

The following week, back at $2.99, I sold over 5,000 more copies. For the next two weeks, sales settled in at 75 to 100 copies a day, and I was still delighted. Readers were leaving nice comments on the Amazon site, and some folks were now buying the paperback version at its $14.95 retail price. After almost a month, my listing disappeared from the "top 100 Bestsellers," but the book was still listed at somewhere between # 40 and #60 on the Historical Fiction bestseller lists.

How long will the run last? I have no idea, but in that one month I paid all the production costs of this book, and have enough in the bank to completely finance my next book. I can start to turn a profit with the first copy. Sales have now steadied out at around 100 to 200 copies a week, but that is still providing a lovely constant stream of income. Can't ask for more!

⌒⌒⌒

Kindle Free Books: The New Public Library

Someone asked me recently about the first book I ever published. How big a thrill was it? Honestly, I remember a bit of disappointment. Maybe I had been expecting too much—trumpets and fanfares would have been nice. Instead, the delivery guy dumped a box on my office floor, mumbling about how hard my office was to find. (Yeah, well, I admit it was in the basement of the Physics building, not where one would expect to find a "published" professor of medieval history.)

Gamely I unpacked that box and trotted off to the dean's office to present him with the first copy. He looked at the cover, didn't bother to open it, and said, "That's nice, Carolyn. But what have you written lately?" I was crushed. Little did I realize that that phrase—what have you written lately?—would be the recurring chorus of the rest of my life.

When did the thrill come? Not until a couple of years later. I was in Washington, DC, helping to judge projects for the National Endowment for the Humanities. On the weekend, my husband and I went to the Library of Congress, where I headed straight for the card catalog (no electronic searches in those days) and hunted for my name. And there it was, among those millions of other cards: *The Dilemma of Arnulf of Lisieux*, by Carolyn Poling Schriber. Gasp. I was a real author. In a real library.

I tend to forget that feeling these days, with several books to my credit and little need to visit a library, thanks to the Internet. But libraries, whether they are stately edifices or dingy back rooms or computer screens, have always been an important—maybe the only important—link between an author and a reader. And it's that connection that matters—the moment when an author says something important and a reader gets it.

I needed to remember that fact recently. I was at a meeting among friends and colleagues. The other attendees were not academics this time, but good people, dedicated to serving their communities and helping those in need. In a casual conversation, someone mentioned that my book, *Beyond All Price*, had become the number-one bestseller among Amazon's free Kindle editions of historical fiction. What did the other listeners hear? "Free." One fellow shook his head in pity: "That's nice, Carolyn, but those are all copies you gave away. They're worthless. You didn't make a cent on them." I don't remember what I mumbled in response. But here's what I should have said:

"Worthless? More than thirty thousand people now have my book in their hands. It didn't cost them anything, but they asked for it because they wanted to read it. How is that different than a patron going into the town library and asking to borrow an interesting book? A library buys one book and passes it around until the cover falls off. The author may earn a few cents (although I never earned a dime from *The Dilemma of Arnulf of Lisieux*), but the readers get it for free. Money doesn't bestow any value on a book. The only thing that gives a book value is the moment when a reader picks it up and "gets" what the author has to offer – whether that's new knowledge, an emotional experience, inspiration, understanding, or pure entertainment."

So, in answer to all the critics of electronic books, as well as to all those who judge an item's worth by dollar signs, I suggest that

Kindle's free book offerings are the equivalent of a great public library. Both provide free books to readers. Sure, a reader still has to pick and choose among the offerings. Some books will be wonderful and some will be trash. But it matters that they are free and accessible to millions of people who would not otherwise be able to read them.

My own moment in the sun lasted for several weeks, but it gradually faded. Amazon seldom leaves a book on the free list for more than a week, so the price of my book jumped to $2.99, and sales fell. *Beyond All Price* disappeared from the bestseller lists, although the label stuck, at least for a while. What will last even longer? The readers who connect with me, if only for a moment, make the writing process worthwhile. I will remember them longer than those who paid for the book to be polite and left it unopened on a shelf.

∽∾∾

The Elusive Amazon Algorithm

I've seen a few people try to explain how Amazon arrives at its sales rankings, but in the end most give up, because no explanation seems to fit. It's a bit like trying to pick up raw egg white with your fingers. It's there; you can see it; but it constantly escapes your grasp. One reason is that the rankings change every hour. No explanation will be fully accurate long enough to write it down.

Here's what we do know, and what we don't. It seems entirely possible that Amazon now carries over ten million books, although less than six million have ever sold a copy. Once the first copy of a book sells, the book gets a ranking, and that ranking now starts out at somewhere around #6,000,000. We don't know exact numbers because books are constantly being added and withdrawn. The same is true for the number of Kindle editions. There are over 900,000 of them, and the numbers are growing every minute.

It is fairly clear that the rankings are based on number and frequency of sales, not on price. The frequency appears to be

173

more important than the numbers. If that were not so, the Bible would be #1 and stay there. It's not, and neither is *The Works of Shakespeare*, although those two books have outsold anything you and I can ever hope to do. Instead, some think that the Amazon ranking depends most heavily on "What's Hot, Right Now."

A book that sells ninety copies within an hour will shoot right to the top of the bestseller list, but it will have to keep on selling ninety copies an hour to stay there. As long as it does so, it will outrank a book that has sold 900 copies in the past twenty-four hours (that one was only selling at a rate of thirty-seven per hour.) And yes, that means that a clever author can manipulate the rankings by asking every friend he knows to order the book at noon on the same day. The trouble with that plan is that the author will run out of friends eventually, and then the high ranking falls with a thud, maybe by two o'clock.

Some other factors enter into the equation as well. Hourly and daily sales are more important than weekly sales, and weekly sales are much more important than monthly ones. That's where the mysterious formulas come into play. The rankings also seem to be affected by the number of reviews your book gets, the number of stars those reviewers award, and, to a lesser degree, by the number of "likes" on those new buttons.

There are probably other factors as well. No two books ever hold the same rank, so there have to be many ways to identify differences among 6,000,000 books. If you watch the rankings closely, you may see that Amazon responds to a high sales rate by putting the book on one of its recommended lists: "Best Books of the Year or Month," "Fall/Winter/Spring/Summer Reading Lists," "Best sellers in . . ." "What's Hot," "Movers and Shakers." These lists go on and on, and they become cause rather than effect. Many Amazon customers rely on those lists to pick their books for them. If Amazon lists your book somewhere, your figures jump, thus perpetuating your sales position. If Amazon decides to take you off the list, sales drop, and your rankings follow suit, proving that they were correct in taking the off the recommended list.

It's all an enormous game, which you need to remember before you get caught up in it. You can manipulate the rankings to some extent by lowering the price of your book Lower cost does translate into more sales at some point, although even the experts are not sure where that point lies. Free books, as I've demonstrated above, can turn you into a best seller, but don't plan on getting rich.

☙ ❧

The Price of Success

Along with the story of my book sales suddenly going viral goes the question of my reaction to the events. Honestly? I experienced equal parts of excitement, greed, disbelief, and sheer panic. I went into the experiment not really believing anything would happen. And when Smashwords distributed only forty-one copies of the book, I was sure the whole idea was ridiculous. I checked several times, and found that Amazon had not lowered my price. Meh!

Then I opened my KDP Reports page one day—and refused to believe what I saw. It was noon on a Tuesday, and it was showing the sale of over 4000 books that day. I remember pointing it out to my husband and saying, "It's a mistake. It has to be. Selling that many books would be disastrous for our income tax." Well, yes and no. The figures were not a mistake, but the price had dropped to $0.00—so no tax problems to worry about.

I got nothing done the rest of the week. I was mesmerized and immobilized by watching the numbers climb. Periodically I took a screen picture of the Kindle Best-sellers list, so I could prove that it all really happened. About midweek, I started putting the bestseller figures on my website, figuring that I needed to take advantage of the momentum. Then I took them down again because I didn't want to brag. Then I put them up again—back and forth, with no idea how to leverage what was happening into a long-term marketing tool.

So what did I learn from the experience?

There may be no limits to human greed and no top limit to "enough." When I sold 4,000 copies, I wanted to reach 5,000, then 6,000, then 7,000. When I was #15 on the Amazon Bestseller list, I wanted a place in the top ten. And when I was #4, I scowled at the first three and wondered what it would take to topple them off their perches. (Never mind that the other three were hardback bestsellers on *The New York Times* lists and backed by big-name publishing houses, while my little paperback was self-published.) I had never thought of becoming a "bestseller," but once there, I didn't want to give it up.

All success is relative. In May, I was thrilled to sell eight books in a single week; in August, I was disappointed and discouraged when sales fell from 5,000 a day to 700 a day—and then from 700 a day to 75 a day. What would have been wild success in May felt like total failure in August. Even now, I'm embarrassed by that reaction.

Everything comes with a price. Once Amazon removed me from the "free" listing, I started to make money. The sudden realization that I had thousands of dollars coming in as royalties meant potential disaster for our family finances. Off we went— first to a financial advisor to look at what the income changes meant in terms of our overall financial picture—then to hire an accountant who could take over a suddenly-complicated income tax situation—and finally to the bank to re-open a separate business account and apply for a business credit card to keep book money separate from everyday living expenses. Like it or not, I had to quit gloating over my "literary" success and start thinking like a hard-hearted business woman, even if that meant laying out more money to pay for expert assistance.

The changes scared me. They still do. I have long quoted the advice, "Be careful what you wish for." No matter, I was totally unprepared for this sudden fame, and my initial reactions were not among my finest moments. I hope I've learned enough from the experience to keep from repeating my self-absorption and greediness.

At least, now, I am back at work on a new book, with finances in better shape than they were several months ago, and I am able at last to take real satisfaction in knowing that *Beyond All Price* has brought reading pleasure to others. Those are important benefits, ones that last longer than book rankings or royalty payments.

Made in the USA
Charleston, SC
16 January 2012